Nigeria

A SURVEY BY THE

Africa Governance Monitoring and Advocacy Project (AfriMAP)

Open Society Initiative for West Africa (OSIWA)

Open Society Media Program (OSMP)

OPEN SOCIETY
FOUNDATIONS

Written by:
Akin Akingbulu (researcher) and Hendrik Bussiek (editor)

Published by:
Open Society Initiative for West Africa

ISBN: 978-1-920489-00-7
ISBN (Ebrary): 978-1-920489-63-2
ISBN (MyiLibrary): 978-1-920489-64-9
ISBN (Adobe PDF digital edition): 978-1-920489-65-6

For more information contact:
AfriMAP
President Place
1 Hood Ave/148 Jan Smuts Ave
Rosebank
South Africa

P.O. Box 678
Wits, 2050
Johannesburg
South Africa

www.afrimap.org
www.osisa.org

Layout and printing:
COMPRESS.dsl, South Africa

Distributed by
African Minds
4 Eccleston Place, Somerset West, 7130, South Africa
info@africanminds.co.za
www.africanminds.co.za

ORDERS:
African Books Collective
PO Box 721, Oxford OX1 9EN, UK
orders@africanbookscollective.com
www.africanbookscollective.com

Contents

Acronyms

ACHPR	African Commission on Human and Peoples' Rights
ACHPR	African Commission on Human and Peoples' Rights
AIT	Africa Independent Television
ALTON	Association of Licenced Telecommunication Operators of Nigeria
AMARC	World Association of Community Radio Broadcasters
ASCON	Administrative Staff College of Nigeria
AU	African Union
BON	Broadcasting Organizations of Nigeria
CFS	Centre for Free Speech
CMC	Central Management Committee
COM	Committee of Management
DLI	Distance Learning Institute
ECOWAS	Economic Community of West African States
EFCC	Economic and Financial Crimes Commission
FEC	Federal Executive Council
FOI	Freedom of Information
FRCN	Federal Radio Corporation of Nigeria
IBAN	Independent Broadcasting Association of Nigeria
ICCPR	International Covenant on Civil and Political Rights
ICPC	Independent Corrupt Practices and other Related Offences Commission
IMS	Institute for Media and Society
INEC	Independent National Electoral Commission
IPC	International Press Centre
ITU	International Telecommunications Union
N	Naira
NAN	News Agency of Nigeria
NBC	National Broadcasting Commission
NBS	Nigerian Broadcasting Service
NCC	Nigerian Communications Commission
NEEDS	National Economic Empowerment and Development Strategy
NEPA	National Electric Power Authority
NGE	Nigerian Guild of Editors
NIG	Nigeria internet Group
NIM	Nigerian Institute of Management
NITDA	National Information Technology Development Agency

NLC	Nigeria Labour Congress
NPAN	Newspapers Proprietors Association of Nigeria
NTA	Nigerian Television Authority
NUJ	Nigeria Union of Journalists
OAU	Organisation of African Unity
PHCN	Power Holding Company of Nigeria
PIWA	Panos Institute West Africa
RATTAWU	Radio, Television, Theatre and Allied Workers Union
SIEC	State Independent Electoral Commission
UNDP	United Nations Development Programme
UNESCO	United Nations Educational, Scientific and Cultural Organisation
VON	Voice of Nigeria

Foreword

The report is the result of research that started in 2008 with the aim of collecting, collating and writing up information about regulation, ownership, access, performance as well as prospects for public broadcasting reform in Africa. The Nigeria report is part of an eleven-country survey of African broadcast media. The main reason for conducting the research is to contribute to Africa's democratic consolidation.

Many African countries have made significant gains in building democratic systems of governance that are based on popular control of decision-making and in which citizens are treated as equals. Availability and access to information by a greater number of citizens is a critical part of a functioning democracy and a country's development. The role of a public broadcaster as a vehicle through which objective information and diverse perspectives are transmitted into the public domain cannot be overstated.

A number of countries are currently undertaking public broadcasting reforms that aim to improve service delivery and accountability to citizens. Such reforms draw from evolving African and global standards regarding media and broadcast media in particular. The survey instrument that was developed in consultation with media experts from Africa and other parts of the world is largely based on agreements, conventions, charters and declarations regarding media that have been developed at regional and continental levels in Africa.

The survey of broadcast media in Africa was initiated by two projects of the Open Society Institute (OSI), the Africa Governance Monitoring and Advocacy Project (AfriMAP) and the Open Society Institute Media Program, working with the African members of the Soros Foundation Network – in West Africa, the Open Society Initiative for West Africa (OSIWA). The research was carried out by Akin Akingbulu, a media/communication consultant and Executive Director of the Institute for Media and Society in Lagos/Nigeria, and edited by Hendrik Bussiek, a media consultant with extensive broadcasting experience in Africa and globally.

It is our hope that the research will clear some of the misconceptions about public broadcasters. In its simplest definition a 'public broadcasting service' is a broadcaster that serves the public as a whole and is accountable to the public as a whole. Yet in most instances what is referred to as a public broadcaster is in fact a state broadcaster. This research aims to help the process of aiding the transformation of Africa's public broadcasters into media worthy of the name.

Ozias Tungwarara
Director, AfriMAP

Introduction

The survey on public broadcasting in Africa starts from the premise that development and democracy cannot thrive without open and free public space where all issues concerning people's lives can be aired and debated and which gives them room and opportunity to participate in decision-making. Nobel Prize laureate Amartya Sen describes democracy as 'governance by dialogue' and broadcasters are ideally placed to facilitate this dialogue by providing the space for it – if their services are accessible, independent, credible and open to the full spectrum of diverse views.

Following from this premise, the key objective of the survey is to assess whether and to what extent the various forms of broadcasting on our continent can and do create such a free public space, with special attention given to those services which call themselves 'public'. A total of eleven country reports look closely at the current status of broadcasting in Benin, Cameroon, Kenya, Mali, Mozambique, Namibia, Nigeria, South Africa, Uganda, Zambia and Zimbabwe.

Following from this premise, the key objective of the survey is to assess whether and to what extent the various forms of broadcasting on our continent can and do create such a free public space, with special attention given to those services which call themselves 'public'. A total of eleven country reports look closely at the current status of broadcasting in Benin, Cameroon, Kenya, Mali, Mozambique, Namibia, Nigeria, South Africa, Uganda, Zambia, and Zimbabwe.

While this survey may be unprecedented in its scope and depth, it does feed into ongoing discussions among broadcasters, civil society and politicians in Africa on the nature and mandate of genuine public broadcasting. Reform efforts are under way in a number of countries. And at least on paper there is already broad consensus on the need to open up the airwaves to commercial and community broadcasters and for state broadcasters to be transformed into truly public broadcasting services. The Declaration of Principles on Freedom of Expression in Africa adopted by the African Union's Commission on Human and Peoples' Rights in 2002, for example, says 'a State monopoly over broadcasting is not compatible with the right to freedom of expression' and demands that 'state and government controlled broadcasters should be transformed into public service broadcasters accountable to the public'. This document and other regional policy declarations serve as major benchmarks for this survey.

In particular, these African documents inform the vision and mandate of public broadcasting as understood in this study.[1] This vision can be summarised as follows:

- to serve the overall public interest and be accountable to all strata of society as represented by an independent board;
- to ensure full respect for freedom of expression, promote the free flow of information and ideas, assist people to make informed decisions and facilitate and strengthen democracy.

The public service broadcasters' mandate is:

- to provide access to a wide range of information and ideas from the various sectors of society;
- to report on news and current affairs in a way which is not influenced by political, commercial or other special interests and therefore comprehensive, fair and balanced (editorial independence);
- to contribute to economic, social and cultural development in Africa by providing a credible forum for democratic debate on how to meet common challenges;
- to hold those in power in every sector of society accountable;
- to empower and inspire citizens, especially the poor and marginalised, in their quest to improve the quality of their lives;
- to provide credible and varied programming for all interests, those of the general public as well as minority audiences, irrespective of religious beliefs, political persuasion, culture, race and gender;
- to reflect, as comprehensively as possible, the range of opinions on matters of public interest and of social, political, philosophical, religious, scientific and artistic trends;
- to promote the principles of free speech and expression as well as of free access to communication by enabling all citizens, regardless of their social status, to communicate freely on the airwaves;

---

1   Apart from the African Commission's Declaration of Principles on Freedom of Expression, these are the African Charter on Broadcasting 2001 as well as the 1995 policy document 'On The Move' and 2007 draft policy paper 'Now is the Time' by the Southern African Broadcasting Association, in which state/public broadcasters in southern Africa commit themselves to the aim of public broadcasting.

- to promote and develop local content, for example through adherence to minimum quotas;
- to provide universal access to their services, with their signal seeking to reach all corners of the country.

Other broadcasting services can – in one way or the other – also fulfill aspects of this mandate, and the survey, therefore, looks at them as well in order to assess their contribution to the creation of a public space.

The facts, figures and informed assessments presented in the survey will, it is hoped, provide a nuanced picture of where broadcasting in Africa at present stands between 'His Master's Voice' of old and the envisaged public broadcasting service of the future. This information should provide a sound basis for advocacy work, both among decision-makers and civil society as a whole.

The report starts out with a comprehensive audit of existing media laws and other legislation with an impact on freedom of expression and a critical in-depth assessment of the legal and regulatory framework in which broadcasting presently operates. This is followed by a detailed study of the state broadcaster – its organisation, its finances, its policies, the content it offers.

In September 2010 a draft report was publicly presented at a round table meeting in Nigeria's capital Abuja, attended by participants from public and private broadcasting stations, media associations and other civil society organisations. Participants discussed the findings, corrected assumptions and errors, debated and endorsed conclusions and recommendations and made a number of additions which were incorporated into the final version.

The researcher and editor would like to express their gratitude to all those who contributed by sharing their information and insights and providing valuable feedback and constructive criticism.

Hendrik Bussiek

1
Country Facts

1 Government

Nigeria returned to civilian government in 1999 after elections that ended 16 years of military rule. The First and Second Republics (1960 to 1966 and 1979 to 1983) had both been overturned by military coups; in some cases the military regimes that resulted were themselves ousted by fresh coups. The Third Republic is established under a written constitution, the fourth since the country's independence in 1960.[2]

The 1999 Constitution provides for government to be structured in three tiers: federal, state and local. There are 36 states and 774 local governments, six of them located in the Federal Capital Territory.

The country operates under a presidential system of government, featuring the principles of federalism and separation of powers. The executive powers of the federation are vested in the president, assisted by a vice-president and ministers. A governor heads at the state level, and a chairman at the local government level. The vice-president and deputy governors are elected directly on the same ticket with their principal.

Federal legislative powers are vested in an elected bi-cameral National Assembly consisting of a Senate and a House of Representatives. The Senate has a membership of 109, based on a quota formula of three members per state and one from the federal capital territory. A total of 360 members sit in the House of Representatives, with the number of constituencies determined by the size of the population of each state. The state and local governments each have a unicameral legislature.

The Constitution splits responsibility for different thematic areas between the federal and state levels of government: the federal government has wider and stronger

---

2   After the first founding document, new constitutions were adopted in 1963, 1979 and 1989, although the 1989 Constitution never entered into force.

powers for legislative and control purposes than the states. In general, the executive branch of government dominates and constrains the legislature across the three tiers, preventing appropriate institutional expression of legislative power.

Nigeria is a multi-party state. The Constitution provides for the holding of elections every four years at the same time for federal- and state-level elected officials and representatives. It establishes three types of election management bodies: the Independent National Electoral Commission (INEC), which registers political parties and conducts national and state elections, along with other functions; the State Independent Electoral Commissions (SIEC), set up by each state and in charge of the conduct of local government elections; and Election Tribunals which adjudicate disputes arising from elections. The INEC is appointed by the president subject to confirmation by the Senate; state governors appoint the SIECs subject to confirmation by each state's House of Assembly. The president of the Court of Appeal appoints Election Tribunals, in consultation with the chief judge of a state, the Grand Kadi of the Sharia Court of Appeal of the state or the president of the Customary Court of Appeal of the state, as the case may be.

Only political parties can sponsor candidates for elections. As a condition for registration, parties are required to have national spread in membership and structures, and cut across ethnic and religious boundaries. Nigeria is a multi-party state. Three political parties participated in the 1999 elections, 27 more were registered for 2003 and a total of 50 for the 2007 elections.

Judicial powers reside in a set of courts, with the Supreme Court of Nigeria at the top of the hierarchy. Lower courts are the Court of Appeal, Federal High Court, High Court of the Federal Capital Territory, and Sharia Court of Appeal of the Federal Capital Territory, Abuja. (Sharia and Customary Courts have jurisdiction over Islamic and customary matters respectively.)

The president appoints judges to these federal courts on the recommendation of the National Judicial Council. Only the heads of courts (chief justice – Supreme Court, president of Court of Appeal, chief judge of the Federal High Court, chief judge of Federal Capital Territory, Abuja, Grand Kadi of the Sharia Court of Appeal, president of the Customary Court of Appeal) are also subject to confirmation by the Senate.

At the entry level in the various states are the magistrate/district courts and customary/area/Sharia courts. The second tier is made up of a High Court, Sharia Court of Appeal and Customary Court of Appeal. Appointments of judges to these structures are made by the state governor on the recommendation of the National Judicial Council. The confirmation of the State House of Assembly is required in the case of the heads of these bodies. The executive branch of government has control over the funding of the judiciary.

2   Balance of powers

Nigerians welcomed the return of civil rule with much excitement and expectation in 1999. Today, however, it appears that not much has changed. Accountability and transparency in governance have still not gained a firm foothold. There have been many incidents of corruption at all levels of government over the past decade. Party-building, and institution-building in general, have received limited attention from political players. Parties in government dominate political life and office-holders seek to hold on to their jobs and powers. The executive branch of government dominates and constrains the legislature across the three tiers, preventing appropriate institutional expression of legislative power.

Nigerians feel short changed. And many civil institutions have been studying this situation. A series of four Afrobarometer Surveys in Nigeria conducted in 2000, 2001, 2003, and 2005 has provided a summary on the changing Nigerian attitudes since the 1999 return of civilian governments as follows:

> Nigerians are broadly discouraged by the performance of their political system, and do not generally believe that they have reaped the 'dividends' of democracy. Nonetheless, a large majority of Nigerians continue to prefer democratic government over all other options, and many Nigerians remain patient about the anticipated benefits of the democratic system. Further, Nigerians are most critical of the government of the day, and relatively less discouraged by the performance of the general regime of democracy. These popular attitudes suggest that Nigeria's new democracy remains fragile, and suffers a growing deficit of popular confidence. However, Nigerians are not ready to abandon the democratic system for non-democratic alternatives such as military rule or a domineering presidency.[3]

3   Basic socio-economic data

The national census of 2006[4] put the country's population at 140 million, with Kano and Lagos states ranking highest, each with over 9 million people.[5] Previous counts in 1963 and 1991 had resulted in population figures of 53 million and 89 million respectively. In general, the census data are not regarded as reliable.

There are several hundred ethnic groups and languages, the biggest of them being

---

3   P. Lewis, 'Performance and Legitimacy in Nigeria's New Democracy', Afrobarometer Briefing Paper no. 46, July 2006, p.2.
4   The Constitution provides for a population census every ten years.
5   National Bureau of Statistics, Annual Abstract of Statistics 2008, accessed from: http://www.nigerianstat.govt.ng.

the Hausa/Fulani, Igbo, Yoruba and Ijaw. English, which was inherited from colonial Britain, is the official language. Major religions are Christianity, Islam and indigenous faiths. Accurate data on proportions are not available. The National Population Commission removed religion from the 2006 census.

Nigeria is endowed with an abundance of natural and other resources. Before and immediately after independence in 1960, the economy was sustained mainly by agriculture in which crops such as cocoa, groundnuts, rubber and palm produce were major export earners. But, following the discovery of oil in the late 1950s, the country gradually became almost completely dependent on oil revenues. Nigeria was, until recently, the top oil producer in Africa; it has now been overtaken by Angola. Oil accounts for over 90 per cent of the country's export revenue and more than 80 per cent of total government income.

The near-total focus on oil and the wanton mismanagement of this resource has led to a decline in local agriculture and industry. Basic staple food items for which Nigeria used to be a major exporter are now imported. The nation's GDP per capita officially stood at US$ 1 118 in 2007 and the annual growth rate over the period 1990–2007 at 1.1 per cent.[6]

In recent years, particularly since 2003, the government has begun to implement some economic reforms. It introduced the National Economic Empowerment and Development Strategy (NEEDS), a programme designed for poverty reduction and better fiscal management. It also embarked on the privatisation of several state agencies, including refineries, and the deregulation of the pricing of refined and imported fuel.

The country has a road network of about 193 000 km, which carries more than 90 per cent of domestic passengers and freight; inland navigable waterways of about 3 000 km and a coastline of about 852 km. There are 3 505 km of railways, mostly single-track gauge, distributed between two (west-to-north and east-to-north) lines. Airports number about 70, four of which handle international flights.

Lofty objectives have been articulated for education. Section 18 of the 1999 Constitution, for instance, provides that government 'shall strive to eradicate illiteracy' and 'shall as and when practicable provide free, compulsory and universal primary education, free secondary education, free university education; and [a] free adult literacy programme'. The reality is that the general adult literacy rate in 2007 stood at 72 per cent, 80.1 per cent for males and 64.1 per cent for females.[7]

The level of commitment to the development of the health sector is revealed in the expenditure deployed there: 3.5 per cent of the total government expenditure is spent

---

6   Human Development Report 2009 – http/hdrstats.undp.org/countries/data/sheet/ accessed on 15 March 2010).
7   Ibid.

on health.[8] And the outcomes: maternal mortality stands at 800 per 100 000 live births; child mortality at 194 per 1 000 live births; HIV/AIDS prevalence at 4.4 per cent in 2005. Life expectancy is declining: from about 52 years in 2000 to 46.5 years in 2007/2008.[9]

Nigeria was ranked 158th out of 182 countries in the 2009 Human Development Index of the United Nations Development Programme (UNDP).[10]

4 Main challenges

Nigeria's journey to recovery and sustainable development is littered with formidable challenges. Among these are:

4.1 Corruption and waste

Transparency and accountability have found it difficult to permeate the conduct of government business. Corruption has become institutionalised at all levels. Members of successive governments have stolen enormous proportions of Nigeria's wealth. According to Dapo Olorunyomi, director at the Economic and Financial Crimes Commission (EFCC), the country lost at least US$ 380 billion to corruption and waste between 1960 and 1999.[11] The outcome is that despite Nigeria's rich human and natural endowments, her future development and stability remain threatened by different forms of corruption. Justice Emmanuel Ayoola, the chair of the Independent Corrupt Practices and other Related Offences Commission (ICPC), one of the anti-corruption agencies established in the past few years, summarised the magnitude of the challenge: 'No society can achieve anything near its potential if corruption becomes a full-blown career. It has become systematic and endemic in our society.'[12]

Accompanying the regime of corruption in Nigeria is the culture of profligacy, characterised mainly by a disdain for maintenance work and lack of attention regarding opportunities with huge economic prospects.

---

8 Ibid.
9 Ibid.; Prof. Babatunde Oshotimehin, chair, National Council for the Control of AIDS (interview) in *The Punch*, 22 Jan 2008.
10 Human Development Report, op.cit.
11 Interview on 7 January 2008.
12 'ICPC recruits Nigerians to spy on governors, LG bosses', *Nigerian Tribune* (online edition), 10 August 2007 (http://www.tribune.com.ng/10082007/news/news3.html), accessed on 23 August 2007.

4.2 Electoral/succession processes

The Nigerian political class has demonstrated a preference for either disrespect for term limits or the acquisition of political mandates by fraudulent means. An attempt by the immediate past president to amend the 1999 Constitution to allow him a third term in office created a national controversy, heated the polity and failed. Elections are often associated with tension, crisis and violence. 'The result is that the outcome of elections has been the subversion of the democratic process rather than its consolidation,' said Jibrin Ibrahim, director of the Centre for Democracy and Development.[13] In recent times, Election Petition Tribunals have declared the elections of office holders in governorship, legislative and other positions invalid on account of electoral malpractices. A former chair of the Independent National Electoral Commission (INEC), Dr Abel Guobadia, explained part of the picture:

> Today, though political parties as required by law, cut across ethnic boundaries, party allegiance for most is only secondary to ethnic allegiances. In many areas, where some political parties have influence, elections amount to ethnic contests for power rather than victory at the polls through presentation of superior development programmes and manifestos.[14]

Reports by domestic and international election observers have in every election since 1999 noted extremely serious flaws in the electoral process, such that the government lacks democratic legitimacy at all levels.

4.3 Poverty and lack of basic public services

The country's population continues to increase, the education sector and other skill-building institutions continuously turn out graduates, but there are fewer and fewer job opportunities. The quality of education provided has also deteriorated. There is high unemployment and under-employment, particularly among the youth. This increases the poverty level and has become one of the underlying factors for the eruption and escalation of conflicts in many parts of the country. Most Nigerians face an enormous struggle just to secure the basic necessities of life such as food, healthcare and shelter. Only 48 per cent of Nigerians have access to clean water. Electricity and transport infrastructure are also in poor condition, hampering private economic activity.

13   See Jibrin Ibrahim, Nigeria's 2007 elections: The Fitful Path to Democratic Citizenship, United States Institute of Peace, Jan 2007, p.3.
14   A. Guobadia,'Federal Republic of Nigeria – Election Administration', paper presented at the conference on 'Improving the Quality of Election Management', New Delhi, India, 24–26 February 2005.

4.4 Security of the state and of the people

Nigeria has experienced security threats and upheavals of various dimensions since independence in 1960. Among them are at least eight military coups and a three-year civil war. Since the return to civilian rule, inter-communal violence has threatened the stability of government in several local government areas or states. Thousands of Nigerians have died in such violence, while several million have been internally displaced. Everywhere in Nigeria armed robbery is a serious problem.

4.5 Resource control and the state of the Niger Delta

The 1999 Constitution and several pieces of legislation vest the control of natural resources such as oil and other minerals in the federal government. The Constitution also provides that 13 per cent of oil revenues should be returned on a 'derivation basis' to the states where they are generated. These provisions are challenged by residents of the oil-producing region of the Niger Delta in particular, where there has been agitation for higher shares of the oil revenues and stronger presence of government in terms of provision of social infrastructure, among other demands. In recent years, political movements for a greater benefit from oil production to be returned to the people have increasingly mutated into criminal activity, as militant groups sabotage oil production facilities, take hostages, and generally disrupt economic activity. A large percentage of oil production is either stolen on a daily basis, with grave consequences for the national economy. There is abundant evidence that senior politicians and armed forces personnel also benefit from these activities.

4.6 Problematic federalism

Nigeria is supposed to be operating a federal system, but several provisions of the 1999 Constitution and other laws concentrate too many powers in the federal government and constrain the state and local governments in many areas. Some examples: the police force is a federal agency and efforts to establish state-controlled police services have been unsuccessful; states cannot create new local governments without recourse to the federal government; whatever natural resources exist in states and local governments, the control is vested in the federal government. According to Itse Sagay, law professor and senior advocate of Nigeria, this situation creates 'a federal government that is a leviathan, overwhelming everybody with its political power and all the resources of the country'; 'too much centralism ... is suffocating Nigeria, and that is why we are not developing'.[15]

4.7 Undermining of national institutions

The independence of the judiciary and constitutionally established institutions has been weakened and is under constant threat from political actors. Legislatures have failed to fulfill their mandates in many places because executive office holders have 'pocketed' them. The electoral bodies, the INEC and the state commissions, have not been able to conduct credible electoral processes partly because they lack independence. Their composition/nomination and funding are constitutional responsibilities of the executive. Anti-corruption bodies have received public applause for punishing theft of public resources and recovering huge amounts of stolen funds as well as for castigating the old culture of impunity. But they operate under tremendous pressure exerted by office holders who themselves at different times are facing legal action for alleged corrupt practices.

4.8 Mono-product economy and the 'curse of oil'

Many of the sources of Nigeria's problems can be found in its virtually complete dependence on a single source of income: oil. The well-documented problems of a hydrocarbon economy are visited on Nigeria in extreme ways, as the political economy revolves around the distribution of oil revenues and other parts of the polity and economy are neglected. The country has been raking in huge revenues because of price rises in the international market over the past few years, yet these revenues are stolen or dissipated rather than invested in the improvement of the country.

5   The media landscape

The history of modern media of mass communication in Nigeria dates back to 1859 when a newspaper, *Iwe Irohin*, was established by a cleric, Henry Townsend, in Abeokuta, in today's south-west Nigeria. The print media sub-sector has grown tremendously over the past 148 years.

There are over 100 newspapers and magazines, most of them owned by private commercial interests. The *New Nigerian*, originally owned by the governments of the

---

15   See 'Centralism is Suffocating, Killing Nigeria' (interview), *The Guardian*, 3 August 2008, p. 22.

19 northern states and taken over by the federal government in 1976, was transferred back to its original owners in 2006. The plan now is for the paper to be privatised. The federal government divested from the *Daily Times* in 2003 under its privatisation programme.

Many state governments own newspapers whose circulation and coverage are limited to their states and neighbouring towns.

The biggest and most vibrant newspapers and magazines are located in the Lagos area, the country's commercial capital.

The most influential newspapers include *The Punch, The Guardian, Vanguard, Daily Trust, ThisDay, Nigerian Tribune, The Nation, The Sun* and *The Daily Independent*. Among the news magazines, *Tell, The News, Newswatch, The Source* and *The Insider* have the strongest influence. Actual circulation figures are not known because Nigerian newspapers and news magazines do not make such information available to the public.

Indigenous language newspapers, which grew remarkably over the past decade, are competing strongly with their English language counterparts. Some circulate to all parts of the country. The most influential ones are *Gaskiya* (Hausa language) and *Alaroye* (Yoruba).

There is one official news agency, the News Agency of Nigeria (NAN), established in 1976 with offices in all states of the country and serving both print and broadcast media. The agency comes under the ministry of information and is supervised by a board appointed by the minister. The act establishing NAN guarantees the agency a monopoly for gathering and disseminating news.

The broadcast sector has expanded in the past ten years of civil rule. Stations owned by the federal government have embarked on fresh expansion programmes: the Federal Radio Corporation of Nigeria (FRCN) is establishing 32 new stations while the Nigerian Television Authority (NTA) is building 95 new stations. These are to operate with full-blown programming. All the state governments operate radio stations, and most run television stations as well.

Since 1993, the regulatory body, the National Broadcasting Commission (NBC), has issued more than 120 private radio, television and cable TV licences.

Geographical coverage of broadcast stations varies according to ownership and mandate. Stations owned by the federal government (e.g. FRCN, NTA) have mandates for nationwide coverage. Those which belong to state governments cover their respective states. The coverage of private stations is not uniform. Some cover just one state, others a group of states. In recent years, a few have moved to establish a network of stations while others have started to service international audiences via digital satellite television (DSTV) arrangements.

According to the National Bureau of Statistics, 88 per cent of households have access to radio (ownership: 72.9 per cent) and 51 per cent to television (ownership: 36.6 per cent).[16]

The number of fixed telephony subscribers stood at about 1.58 million by 2007. Mobile telephony had about 40.4 million subscribers in the same year, giving 66.2 per cent of households access to mobile phones (ownership: 44.3 per cent). Internet services are accessed by 6.5 per cent of households (14.7 in urban and 2.2 per cent in rural areas) and 1.4 per cent of households own a personal computer.[17]

Broadband penetration has been rather slow in Nigeria. One industry source put penetration figures for 2006 at 0.01 per cent. The reason is the cost, which is not generally affordable.

The government has instituted a State Accelerated Broadband Initiative, SABI, which is expected to speed up the deployment of broadband in the country.

It would appear that the new media operations have been more pro-active than their broadcasting counterparts in the unfolding media/ICT convergence scenario.

Except for the FRCN, where four stations stream live audio on the internet, there is no appreciable presence of Nigerian broadcasting stations on the internet. Meanwhile, GSM phone service providers are already deploying 3G technology to provide services which include video/visual services.

The state of access to each of these information and communication channels varies. The average daily newspaper sells for between N 100 (US$ 0.66[18]) and N 200 (US$ 1.32) while the cover price of a news magazine ranges from N 200 (US$ 1.32) to N 300 (US$ 2.00). In comparison, an average loaf of bread sells for N 100 (US$ 0.66). Newspapers are neither a priority nor affordable for large sections of the population.

Access to terrestrial radio and television is free. Prices of radio and TV sets are largely determined by brand or technology. An average radio set sells for about N 5 000 (US$ 33) while a TV set costs at least N 20 000 (US$ 132). In a situation where average income is less than N 118 000 (US$ 780), the price of a TV set is beyond the reach of many people, while radio sets are more affordable.

Recent liberalisation efforts of government have led to tariff reductions in the pay-TV field. In the telephony sector, particularly GSM, competition has brought about a slight decrease in tariffs and the introduction of incentives to subscribers.

Citizens now receive information from a rich variety of media outlets. Radio leads because of its relative affordability, ability to provide information without literacy barriers, and availability to consumers at home and while on the move, such as in cars.

---

16   National Bureau of Statistics, op.cit., 2007 figures.
17   Ibid.
18   N 100 = US$ 0.66 (www.xe.com 15 March 2010).

Television and newspapers are more available to urban-based and relatively higher-income citizens. Business, political and social relations are managed through phone and other services which are readily available.

6   Brief history of broadcasting

Radio broadcasting was introduced in Nigeria in 1932 as an experiment of the empire service of the BBC. Full broadcasting services in the country began with the establishment of the Nigerian Broadcasting Service (NBS) in 1952. The NBS was transformed into the Nigerian Broadcasting Corporation (NBC) in 1956.

Seizing the opportunity of colonial constitutional review which gave federal and regional governments concurrent powers in the ownership of broadcasting stations, the government of the western region established television and radio stations in 1959. The governments of the eastern and northern regions followed suit in 1960 and 1962 respectively. The federal government also set up a television station in 1962.

After the military had overthrown the civilian constitutional government in 1966, it created 12 states to replace the regions as the second tier of government. New states established their own broadcasting stations.

The federal broadcasting corporation, NBC, also began to expand in 1967, building a station in each state. But this was reversed by a policy change in the 1970s. Government ordered the transfer of most NBC stations to the states, with the exception of those in Lagos, Ibadan and Enugu, and added the Kaduna station of the Broadcasting Corporation of Northern Nigeria. It also transformed the NBC into the Federal Radio Corporation of Nigeria (FRCN).

At the same time, the government centralised all federal and state television stations under the control of a new body, the Nigerian Television Authority (NTA).

When the country returned to civilian rule in 1979, state governments exploited a constitutional provision which granted them powers to establish new television stations. Federal radio also expanded its operations through building stations in all states.

The military seized power again and scrapped the new federal radio stations in 1984.

In the mid-1980s. the government embarked on the Structural Adjustment Programme (SAP) which included steps to cut down on state subsidies. This led to the introduction of commercialisation in the state broadcasters – the FRCN and NTA. For the first time, government designed a National Mass Communication Policy which was published in 1990. The policy retained government's monopoly over the broadcasting sector.

In another reversal of policy, government promulgated a decree in 1992 which established a regulatory body, the National Broadcasting Commission (NBC), and opened the door to private participation in the ownership and operation of broadcasting stations.

The NBC began its work in 1993 and issued the first set of licences the same year.

The NTA and FRCN started on a new expansion programme with the setting up of more stations) beginning in 2000/01.

Government initiated a review of the 1990 mass communication policy in 2004, and started to design new policies for community radio development and frequency spectrum management in 2006. These three processes still have to be concluded.

2

Media Legislation and Regulation

1   International, continental and regional standards

Nigeria is party to a number of international and regional legal documents relating to freedom of expression. As a member and key player in continental and regional institutions such as the African Union (AU) and the Economic Community of West African States (ECOWAS), the country is expected to be subject to their governing instruments.

1.1   United Nations

The following instruments of the UN are relevant to freedom of expression:

The United Nations Universal Declaration of Human Rights (adopted in 1948)

The Universal Declaration is not a treaty that is ratified by states and thus legally binding. However, scholars now regard it as either having itself become international customary law or as a reflection of such law.[19] In either case the inclusion of freedom of expression in the declaration implies that even states that have ratified none of the relevant treaties are bound to respect freedom of expression as a human right.

Article 19 of the Declaration deals with the right to freedom of expression:

> Everyone has the right to freedom of opinion and expression; this right includes freedom to hold opinions without interference and to seek, receive and impart information and ideas through any media and regardless of frontiers.

---

19   See, for example, H. Hannum, 'The Status and Future of the Customary International Law of Human Rights: The Status of the Universal Declaration of Human Rights in National and International Law', *Georgia Journal of International and Comparative Law*, 287; H. J. Steiner, P. Alston and R. Goodman, *International Human Rights in Context: Law, Politics, Morals – Texts and Materials*, Oxford: Oxford University Press (third edition), 2007.

International Covenant on Civil and Political Rights (enacted by the United Nations in 1976)
The International Covenant on Civil and Political Rights (ICCPR) is a treaty that elaborates on many of the rights outlined in the Declaration. Nigeria acceded to the Covenant in 1993, but has not incorporated its provisions into domestic law. The Covenant's article 19 declares:

1) Everyone shall have the right to hold opinions without interference;
2) Everyone shall have the right to freedom of expression; this right shall include freedom to seek, receive and impart information and ideas of all kinds, regardless of frontiers, either orally, in writing or in print, in the form of art, or through any other media of his choice.

The Windhoek Declaration on Promoting an Independent and Pluralistic African Press (adopted by the General Assembly of UNESCO in 1991)
The UN Educational, Scientific and Cultural Organisation's (UNESCO) Windhoek Declaration, like other non-treaty documents, has moral authority by representing a broad consensus of the international community on the detailed interpretation of the Universal Declaration and other relevant standards as they relate to the press in Africa.
   Article 9 of the Windhoek Declaration states:

[We] declare that
1) Consistent with article 19 of the Universal Declaration of Human Rights, the establishment, maintenance and fostering of an independent, pluralistic and free press is essential to the development and maintenance of democracy in a nation, and for economic development.
2) By an independent press, we mean a press independent from governmental, political or economic control or from control of materials and infrastructure essential for the production and dissemination of newspapers, magazines and periodicals.
3) By a pluralistic press, we mean the end of monopolies of any kind and the existence of the greatest possible number of newspapers, magazines and periodicals reflecting the widest possible range of opinion within the community.

1.2 African Union

Nigeria is a member of the African Union (AU), whose Constitutive Act states that its objectives include the promotion of 'democratic principles and institutions, popular participation and good governance' (article 3[g]).

The most important human rights standard adopted by the AU, or its predecessor, the Organisation of African Unity (OAU), is:

The African Charter on Human and Peoples' Rights (adopted 27 June 1981)[20]
Nigeria acceded to the Charter in 1983, and domesticated it in national law the same year.[21] Article 9 of the Charter states on freedom of expression:

- Every individual shall have the right to receive information.
- Every individual shall have the right to express and disseminate his opinions within the law.

The African Commission on Human and Peoples' Rights (ACHPR) is the body established under the Charter to monitor and promote compliance with its terms.

Declaration of Principles on Freedom of Expression in Africa (adopted by formal resolution by the ACHPR in 2002)
In 2002, the African Commission adopted this Declaration to provide a detailed interpretation for member states of the AU of the rights to freedom of expression outlined in the African Charter, stating in its article I:

> Freedom of expression and information, including the right to seek, receive and impart information and ideas, either orally, in writing or in print, in the form of art, or through any other form of communication, including across frontiers, is a fundamental and inalienable human right and an indispensable component of democracy.
>
> Everyone shall have an equal opportunity to exercise the right to freedom of expression and to access information without discrimination.

---

20 Organisation of African Unity, *The African Charter on Human and Peoples' Rights*, adopted 27 June 1981, Doc. CAB/LEG/67/3 rev. 5, 21 I.L.M. 58 (1982), entered into force 21 October 1986.
21 African Charter on Human and Peoples' Rights (Ratification and Enforcement) Act (no. 2 of 1983). The status if the African Charter in Nigerian law and its relationship to the constitution was the subject of litigation under the military regimes: in the case of *Abacha and Others v. Fawehinmi* (2001) AHRLR 172 (NgSC 2000), heard under military rule, the Nigerian Supreme Court overruled the Court of Appeal to find that the African Charter could not be superior to the Constitution, but had status as just another piece of national legislation.

It goes on to say in article II:

> No one shall be subject to arbitrary interference with his or her freedom of expression; and
> Any restrictions on freedom of expression shall be provided by law, serve a legitimate interest and be necessary in a democratic society.

The Declaration details how such freedom of expression should be realised. Of particular relevance to this study is the statement regarding public broadcasting (article VI):

> State and government controlled broadcasters should be transformed into public service broadcasters, accountable to the public through the legislature rather than the government, in accordance with the following principles:
> · public broadcasters should be governed by a board which is protected against interference, particularly of a political or economic nature;
> · the editorial independence of public service broadcasters should be guaranteed;
> · public broadcasters should be adequately funded in a manner that protects them from arbitrary interference with their budgets;
> · public broadcasters should strive to ensure that their transmission system covers the whole territory of the country; and
> · the public service ambit of public broadcasters should be clearly defined and include an obligation to ensure that the public receive adequate, politically balanced information, particularly during election periods.

The document also states that freedom of expression 'places an obligation on the authorities to take positive measures to promote diversity' (article II), that community and private broadcasting should be encouraged (article V) and that broadcasting and telecommunications regulatory authorities should be independent and 'adequately protected against interference, particularly of a political or economic nature' (article VII). The Declaration furthermore provides for freedom of access to information and states that 'the right to information shall be guaranteed by law' (article IV).

African Charter on Democracy, Elections and Governance (2007)
This Charter highlights the importance of access to information in a democracy. It states:

[State parties shall] [p]romote the establishment of the necessary conditions to foster citizen participation, transparency, access to information, freedom of the press and accountability in the management of public affairs. (Article 2[10])

State parties shall ... ensure fair and equitable access by contesting parties to state controlled media during elections. (Article 17[3])

Records at the ministry of justice show that Zambia has yet to accede to this Charter.

1.3 Economic Community of West African States

The Treaty Establishing the Economic Community of West African States (1993)

Nigeria is a member of the Economic Community of West African States (ECOWAS). The ECOWAS Treaty, the founding document, was first adopted in 1975 and revised in 1993.

Under article 65 of the Treaty, member states undertake to:

- coordinate their efforts and pool their resources in order to promote the exchange of radio and television programmes at bilateral and regional levels;
- encourage the establishment of programme exchange centres at regional level and strengthen existing programme exchange centres;
- use their broadcasting and television systems to promote the attainment of the objectives of the community.

Under article 66, member states further undertake to:

- maintain within their borders and between one another, freedom of access for professionals of the communication industry and for information sources;
- facilitate exchange of information between their press organs, promote and foster effective dissemination of information within the community;
- ensure respect for the rights of journalists;
- take measures to encourage investment capital, both public and private, in the communication industries in member states;
- modernize the media by introducing training facilities for new information techniques;
- promote and encourage dissemination of information in indigenous languages, strengthening cooperation between national press agencies and developing linkages between them.

ECOWAS Protocol on Democracy and Good Governance (2001)[22]
In 2001 member states of ECOWAS adopted a protocol to the treaty which established standards on good governance to apply in the West Africa region. Heads of state agreed to respect a range of principles relating to free political activity, the rule of law and respect for human rights. One of these principles, set out in section 1.1(k), is that:

> The freedom of the press shall be guaranteed.

1.4 Other documents

African Charter on Broadcasting (2001)
This Charter was adopted by media practitioners and international media and other human rights organisations at a UNESCO conference to celebrate ten years of the Windhoek Declaration. Although it has not been endorsed by any inter-state structures, it represents a consensus of leading African and other international experts on freedom of expression and media.

The Charter specifies, amongst other things, that there should be a three-tier system of broadcasting (public, private and community), demands that '[a]ll state and government controlled broadcasters should be transformed into public service broadcasters', and states that regulatory frameworks should be based on 'respect for freedom of expression, diversity and the free flow of information and ideas'.

2   The Constitution of Nigeria

Two sections of the 1999 Constitution contain the key provisions on freedom of expression and the media.

The 'Right to freedom of expression and the press' is articulated in chapter IV which deals with Fundamental Rights. Section 39(1) states that:

> Every person shall be entitled to freedom of expression, including freedom to hold opinions and to receive and impart ideas and information without interference.

Subsection 2 specifies further:

> Without prejudice to the generality of subsection 1 of this section, every person

---

22 Protocol on Democracy and Good Governance Supplementary To The Protocol Relating to the Mechanism for Conflict Prevention, Management, Resolution, Peacekeeping and Security A/Sp1/12/01.

shall be entitled to own, establish and operate any medium for the dissemination of information, ideas and opinions.

With regard to broadcasting, however, the same subsection goes on to make an important exception:

Provided that no person, other than the government of the Federation or of a state or any other person or body authorized by the President on the fulfillment of conditions laid down by an act of the National Assembly, shall own, establish or operate a television or wireless broadcasting station for any purpose whatsoever.

This section thus empowers the president (and not an independent regulator) to license broadcasters.

Subsection (3) sets out a number of limitations on the right to freedom of expression and the press:

Nothing in this section shall invalidate any law that is reasonably justified in a democratic society –

(a) for the purpose of preventing the disclosure of information received in confidence, maintaining the authority and independence of courts or regulating telephony, wireless broadcasting, television or the exhibition of cinematograph films; or

(b) imposing restrictions upon persons holding office under the Government of the federation or of a state, members of the armed forces of the federation or members of the Nigeria Police Force or other Government security services or agencies established by law.

While subsection 3(a), among others, lays the constitutional basis for the regulation of broadcasting and telecommunications in general, subsection 3(b) allows for laws restricting freedom of expression for civil servants, such as the Official Secrets Act.

Chapter II of the Constitution deals with 'Fundamental Objectives and Directive Principles of State Policy'. These are listed in detail in sections 13 to 21 and range from the overarching goal 'to secure the maximum welfare, freedom and happiness of every citizen on the basis of social justice and equality of status and opportunity', to ensuring that 'all citizens, without discrimination on any group whatsoever, have the opportunity for securing adequate means of livelihood as well as adequate opportunity to secure suitable employment'. The chapter spells out that 'Government shall strive to eradicate illiteracy; and to this end Government shall as and when practicable' provide free education at all levels, and also includes the broad environmental goal to 'protect and improve the environment and safeguard the water, air and land, forest and wild life of Nigeria'.

Section 22 refers specifically to the role of the media in regard to these objectives and principles of state policy:

> The press, radio, television and other agencies of the mass media shall at all times
> be free to uphold the fundamental objectives contained in this chapter and uphold
> the responsibility and accountability of the Government to the people.

The media and citizens in general are known to cherish and actively exercise their freedom of expression in Nigeria. For example, according to a study conducted in 20 countries across the world in 2008, 91 per cent of Nigerian respondents say it is important to have freedom of the media. Other countries where a large proportion of respondents expressed that opinion are the United States (88 per cent), Great Britain (88 per cent), France (80 per cent), Egypt (96 per cent), South Korea (93 per cent) and India (52 per cent). Nigerians have one of the largest majorities rejecting the argument that the government should have the right to restrict media freedom to ensure stability (supported by just 28 per cent), instead expressing themselves in favour of the media having the right to publish news and ideas without government control (71 per cent).[23]

Nigeria ranks second (with 70 per cent) among countries where a majority of citizens would like to see more press freedom. The others are Mexico (75 per cent), China (66 per cent), South Korea (65 per cent), Egypt (64 per cent), the Palestinian Territories (62 per cent), Azerbaijan (57 per cent), Jordan (56 per cent), Indonesia (53 per cent) and Peru (51 per cent).[24]

A series of surveys conducted by Afrobarometer in which Nigerians were asked to assess the present state of fundamental liberties have shown a marked decline in positive perceptions since 2000. While freedom of speech rated a high of about 90 per cent in that year (respondents saying the present system is relatively better), this figure went down to about 85 per cent in 2001, 65 per cent in 2003, and 45 per cent in 2005. Freedom of association and electoral freedom have similar ratings.[25]

This rating is a reflection of the increase in violations of the rights of journalists and the media in general over the past few years. When the military rulers returned to the barracks in 1999, Nigerians hoped that the era of persecution of media workers

---

23 *World Public Opinion on Freedom of the Media*, WorldPublicOpinion.org, 1 May 2008.
24 'More Nigerians want media freedom – Poll', *The Punch*, 17 June 2008.
25 See 'Performance and legitimacy in Nigeria's new democracy', Afrobarometer Briefing Paper no. 46, July 2008, pp. 9–10.

was over and that the new civilian era would be characterised by respect for the constitutional right of freedom of expression as well as a favourable environment for the media to operate. This was not to be.

What looked like sporadic violations in the early period of the present civilian era has gradually grown into a more systematic attack on freedom of expression and the media with diverse manifestations ranging from arrests, detentions and prosecution to closure of media houses and even murder of journalists. Officials of government, including security agencies such as the police and state security service, are responsible for most of these violations, although some proportion is traceable to non-state actors. Types of violations have included the following cases:

- A senior editor of *ThisDay* newspaper, Godwin Agbroko, was murdered by unknown persons in 2006. His killers have never been found.
- Journalists have received death threats from anonymous callers over published or advertised stories (weekly news magazines and weekend issues of newspapers usually advertise major stories of upcoming editions in other newspapers or other titles of the same stable). In one prominent instance, the editors of *Tell*, a leading news magazine, had to petition the head of the police to get protection.
- Denial of accreditation to journalists covering the beat of executive branches of government or legislatures has become common in the past eight years, starting in the Presidential Villa in Abuja in 2002. Government spokespersons cited security and space constraints as reasons, but it was widely known that the affected journalists were from media organisations which had been critical of government. The practice spread to many states, where journalists are declared *persona non grata* in the premises of executive government offices and legislatures. Things got to a point when, in the face of strong industry-wide protests, the National Assembly had to abandon a plan to 'document' correspondents covering its activities. The journalists were to be required to provide information on themselves and their media organisations on printed forms to be designed by the Assembly's administration and used to determine which journalists/media would be allowed to cover its activities.
- Seizures and confiscations of media products and equipment have been reported from many parts of the country. Security operatives have seized consignments of newspapers or news magazines considered offensive by the authorities. In many cases, such raids are carried out on distributors and vendors in various city locations. Photojournalists and TV cameramen have

been victims of the brutality of government officials' security aides who seize and damage their equipment at state functions.

- There have been a number of arbitrary closures. For example, Freedom Radio, a commercial station based in Kano, in the north-west of the country, was closed down following complaints over broadcast content in March 2006 allegedly after a number of callers on phone-in programmes had criticised the then president's bid for the extension of his term of office. The regulatory body, the National Broadcasting Commission, said the handling of some programmes by the station lacked professional maturity, allowing audiences to make unguarded statements tending to overheat the polity and violating the Nigeria Broadcasting Code. Africa Independent Television (AIT), a Lagos-based private outfit, was closed down in October 2005 after it had aired scenes at the site of a plane crash. Detectives in May 2006 shut the offices of *Insider* magazine in the Ogba district of Lagos after the paper had alleged that a state governor was involved in looting state resources and laundering money.
- Arrests, detention and trial of journalists are common. Government continues to charge journalists under the sedition law which has been pronounced unconstitutional by the Court of Appeal in 1983 (see below,). Among the victims of government's use of this law were journalists from *Insider* Magazine, the *Daily Independent* newspaper and Africa Independent Television (AIT). They were charged for reports on alleged corrupt practices in government. Government later dropped the charges.
- Assaults on journalists at public functions have become a frequent occurrence. Intemperate security details seem to enjoy inflicting harm on media professionals on lawful duty.
- Live transmission of foreign news on broadcast stations has been banned.
- Denial of advertising to media houses is a subtle economic weapon used by government agencies and private corporate organisations.

All these incidents have lowered the country's freedom of expression and media rating by international monitors in the past few years.

Table 1: Nigeria's international rating on the Press Freedom Index

Year	Nigeria's position	No. of countries ranked
2002	49	139
2003	103	166
2004	(not ranked)	167
2005	(not ranked)	167
2006	120	168
2007	131	169
2008	131	173

Source: Annual Worldwide Press Freedom Index – Reporters sans Frontiers (2002–2008) – www.rsf.org

3 General media laws and regulations

3.1 Laws and statutory regulation

The Printing Presses (Regulation) Act 1933

This law provides for mandatory registration of printing presses, books and papers. Such registration shall be through a declaration before a magistrate. A new declaration has to be made whenever the operational address changes. The law prescribes a sanction of six months imprisonment or a fine, or both, for failure to make the declaration or for making false statements in it.

The law further provides in section 4(1) that every book or paper printed within the federal territory must bear upon the front page or first and last leaf of every copy, in legible characters in the English language, the name and address of the printer, publisher and the place of publication. The penalty for contravention of this section is a fine or six months imprisonment or both.

A 1964 subsidiary law added more stringent provisions such as allowing the visit of a police officer of or above the rank of an assistant superintendent or an administrative officer to the premises of any press between the hours of 08h00 and 17h00, for the purpose of checking that the provisions of the Act have been carried out.

The Newspaper Act and Newspaper (Amendment) Act 1964

Originally a 1917 colonial ordinance, the Newspaper Act later became part of post-independence legislation. A number of states also have similar laws whose provisions are essentially the same.

The Act provides that before a newspaper is published or printed the proprietor, printer and publisher must:

- Each register an affidavit in the office of the Minster of Information. This affidavit must contain the title and name of the newspaper, description of the house or building where it would be printed and the names and places of abode of the persons intended to be proprietor, printer and publisher.
- Execute and register a bond each in the office of the Minister in the sum of N 500 [in 1964, N 500 was a large amount] with sureties.

Signed copies of each edition of a paper must be delivered to the office of the minister.

The Newspaper (Amendment) Act of 1964 sets out additional requirements:

- Every newspaper which is printed/published outside the Federal Capital Territory but circulates there, must establish an office in Abuja within 2 months from the start of circulation, and the publisher or printer must notify the Minister in writing of his compliance.
- Every newspaper has to appoint an editor, who must also swear to an affidavit as is required of the proprietor and publisher in the principal law.
- It is an offence to authorise for circulation any statement, rumour or report knowing or having reason to believe that such was false. It will not be an admissible defense for an accused to declare that he/she did not know or have reason to believe that the statement, rumour or report was false. He/she can escape punishment only if he/she shows not only that the information was believed to be true but that reasonable measures were taken to verify the accuracy of the story before publication.

The Nigerian Press Council Act 85 of 1992 and the Nigerian Press Council (Amendment) Act 60 of 1999
The law establishes a statutory media regulatory body, the Nigerian Press Council. Its governing body consists of a chairman and sixteen other members, including a secretary. These members are to be drawn from such constituencies as the Nigeria Union of Journalists (NUJ), the Nigerian Guild of Editors (NGE), the Newspapers Proprietors Association of Nigeria (NPAN), the Broadcasting Organisations of Nigeria (BON), educational institutions, the News Agency of Nigeria (NAN), the general public and the federal ministry of information.

While the chairman of this body is to be appointed by the president of the country 'on the recommendation of the minister after due consideration of the submission of the Nigerian Press Organisations' (NUJ, NGE, NPAN), the minister appoints the members 'after an election by or on the nomination of the union, association or other body concerned'. The Press Council reports to the Council of Ministers through the minister of information.

The Press Council's funding sources are government grants and 'such moneys as may be specified by the council to be provided from time to time by the NUJ, NGE, NPAN and BON' (Section 25[b] of Act 85) as well as other funds it might receive in relation to the exercise of its functions.

The Council's duties are to adjudicate on complaints about conduct of the press; to undertake research and documentation; to foster high professional standards; to review developments which are likely to restrict public interest information and free access to the press, and to advise on preventive or remedial measures; and to ensure the protection of journalists' rights and privileges. The Council is vested with powers of sanctions, ranging from a reprimand to ordering the publication of apologies and making recommendations to the NUJ for further disciplinary action.

The law requires registration of all journalists, the procedure being that the NUJ will register and submit a list of registered journalists to the Council. It is an offence to practice journalism without registration.

In order to qualify for registration, a person shall have attended a course of training (in journalism/mass communication) at an institution approved by the NUJ, or shall have acquired not less than five years' experience in journalism before the law came into effect.

In addition, an applicant for registration must satisfy the Council that he/she is of good character, has attained the age of 18 years, has not been convicted of an offence involving fraud and dishonesty, and has a good knowledge of the politics and socio-economic affairs of the country acquired from an approved institution.

If the 1992 law gave rise to a certain amount of criticism, its subsidiary, the 1999 Amendment Act, attracted strong condemnation from stakeholders.

Its controversial provisions include: (i) the powers of the council to register journalists as well as newspapers and magazines annually; (ii) the imposition of sanctions on journalists who fail to register (fine of between N 3 000 (US$ 25) and N 5 000 (US$ 41) or imprisonment for a term not exceeding two years, or both fine and imprisonment); (iii) the replacement of an industry-wide ethical code by a new version to be approved by the council, and (iv) a series of penalties ranging from a fine of N 30 000 (US$ 250) to six months suspension from practice.

A broad section of media stakeholders rejected the Amendment Act and called for its abrogation. Several industry groups, including the Newspapers Proprietors Association of Nigeria (NPAN) went to the Federal High Court sitting in Lagos to challenge government's position and ask for a repeal of the law. In dialogue between the government and stakeholders it was agreed to re-visit the law and produce a version acceptable to the industry.

As it turned out, a commonly acceptable version could not be produced and the whole process got stalled. The administrative structure of the Council (offices and staff) is in place, but industry groups such as the NPAN, NGE and NUJ are refusing to participate in its regulatory activities. There has been no further official word on the issue of registration of journalists. The industry still uses the professional code adopted by the Nigerian Press Organisation (NPO), an umbrella body of industry groups, in 1998. The code deals with issues such as editorial independence, accuracy and fairness, respect for privacy, privilege/non-disclosure of confidential sources, decency in dressing/comportment, use of language, presentation of issues, non-discrimination, and non-acceptance of reward or gratification, among others.

The split between government and the media industry further deepened in 2009. The government strengthened its control of the Council by reconstituting the board and appointing a substantive executive secretary, while the NPAN, for its part, appointed an ombudsman, a retired judge of the Federal Court of Appeal. The ombud is supposed to handle public complaints about alleged professional infractions by members of the association.

In 2010, the Federal High Court decided that the press council laws are inconsistent with Section 39(1) and (2) of the constitution, which guarantee the right to freedom of expression and the press, and are therefore null and void. It granted perpetual injunctions restraining the National Assembly from treating the laws as acts and the executive branch of government from giving effect to any of the provisions of the laws. But the court refused to grant relief sought by the NPAN to the effect that 'the Press' is not one of the matters with respect to which the National Assembly is empowered to make laws. This means that while the present press council laws are unconstitutional and should not be implemented, the National Assembly has constitutional powers to, and could still, enact other laws on press issues.

4   Other laws that impact on media and freedom of expression

4.1   Official Secrets Act (1962)

This law was designed to control access to information held by government. It creates such offences as:

- transmitting classified matter to unauthorised persons;
- obtaining, reproducing and retaining classified official information;
- entering or being in the vicinity of protected places;
- photographing or making sketches or obtaining them of such places; and
- and interfering with persons guarding such places.

The law gives extensive powers to the police – with the consent of the minister of justice – to serve warrants on individuals suspected of having classified official information. It specifies imprisonment of up to 14 years on conviction and a fine or two years imprisonment or both, on summary conviction. Failure to cooperate with a police search order is punishable by imprisonment for up to three months or a fine or both.

4.2 Obscene Publications Act (1961)

The law does not define obscenity but states rather broadly in its section 3(l):

> An article shall be deemed to be obscene for the purpose of this Act if its effect taken as a whole is such as to tend to deprave and corrupt persons who are likely, having regard to all relevant circumstances, to read, see or hear the matter contained or embodied in it.

This further complicates issues because the new key words – 'deprave' and 'corrupt' – are also not defined and, therefore, are open to any kind of interpretation.

The Act specifies penalties for publication of obscene material, namely imprisonment for up to three years or a fine or both. It also provides for the power of search and seizure of publications by the police on the order of a magistrate.

4.3 Sedition

The legislation on sedition, currently provided for in sections 50–52 of the Criminal Code Act (1990), has its roots in the Colonial Criminal Code Act of 1916.

According to section 50(1) a 'seditious publication' is one having a seditious intention. Under section 50(2) a 'seditious intention' is defined as an intention:

> (a) to bring into hatred or contempt or to excite disaffection against the person of the Head of the Federal Military Government, the Governor of a state or the

government or the constitutions of Nigeria or a state as by law established or
against the administration of justice in Nigeria;

(b) to excite Nigerians to attempt to procure the alteration, otherwise than by lawful
means, of any other matter in Nigeria as by law established;

(c) to raise discontent or disaffection among the inhabitants of Nigeria; or

(d) to promote feelings of ill-will and hostility between different classes of the
population of Nigeria.

Upon conviction, the penalty for printing, publishing, selling, offering for sale,
distributing or reproducing any seditious publication is imprisonment for two years
or a fine or both for a first offence, while a subsequent offence attracts imprisonment
for three years. Under the Penal Code (in Northern Nigeria) the offence attracts a
maximum of seven years imprisonment or a fine or both. (In the Federal Capital
Territory and Northern Nigeria the Penal Code applies while in Southern Nigeria the
Criminal Code applies.)

Section 60 of the Criminal Code Act creates an offence for publications which tend
to expose to hatred or contempt heads of other countries in their own countries. The
penalty for this offence is imprisonment for two years.

Section 58 of the Criminal Code Act empowers the minister of justice to prohibit
any publication which in his opinion is 'contrary to public interest'. Importation,
sale, distribution or reproduction of any such prohibited publication is punishable on
conviction with two years imprisonment or N 200 fine or both for a first conviction,
and imprisonment for three years for any subsequent conviction. It is up to the
minister's discretion to define 'public interest'.

'Injurious falsehood' is also an offence provided for in section 59 of the Criminal
Code Act. The law states in subsection 1:

> Any person who publishes or reproduces any statement, rumour or report which is
> likely to cause fear and alarm to the public or to disturb the public peace, knowing
> or having reason to believe that such statement, rumour or report is false, shall be
> guilty of a misdemeanor.

A person convicted under the law is liable to imprisonment of up to three years.

4.4 Defamation

Civil defamation is covered by the Defamation Act of 1961, some state codes and case law. The Act provides, among other things:

- that reference to words shall be construed as including reference to pictures, visual images, gestures and other methods of signifying meaning.
- that the broadcasting of words by means of wireless telegraphy shall be treated as publication in permanent form.
- that justification, fair comment and qualified privilege shall be defences in defamation cases.
- for limitations on privilege such as by forbidding publication of blasphemous or indecent matter. [What constitutes 'blasphemous' and 'indecent' is not defined.]

Section 373 of the Criminal Code deals with criminal defamation. According to section 375, the punishment for publication of defamatory matter is imprisonment for one year, but any person convicted of publishing defamatory matter knowing it to be false will be imprisoned for two years.

In all these pieces of legislation there is no precise definition of defamation. Some determinations, though, can be found in court decisions and legal studies. For example, the Court of Appeal in *Nigerian Television Authority vs Ebenezer Babatope* (1996) defined a defamatory statement as

a statement which is published of and concerning a person and calculated to lower him in the estimation of right-thinking persons or cause him to be shunned or avoided, to expose him to hatred, contempt or ridicule or to convey an imputation on him disparaging or injurious to him in his office, profession, calling, trade or business.[26]

4.5 Access to information

A bill on access to information is before the National Assembly. It seeks to give the public (including the media) access to information held by government agencies. Despite widespread public and media support, the bill is not having an easy ride in the legislature. Opposition by some parliamentarians has slowed its movement in the

---

26 (1996) 4 Nigerian Weekly Law Reports (part 440) 75. Cited in A. Yakubu, *Press Law in Nigeria*, Lagos: Malthouse Press, 1999, p. 45.

House of Representatives. In the Senate, where it was making progress, controversy has erupted (both within and outside the Senate) over the inclusion in the bill of a provision which stipulates that a court must give the go-ahead before an intending user can demand access to any information from a government agency.

5   Jurisprudence

The attitude of courts towards freedom of expression and media has varied from case to case. This would appear to be due to factors which include the state of the law at the time of decision, the direction of precedents (decided cases) and the philosophical approaches of judges (activist or conservative). It is common for higher courts to overturn decisions of lower courts on various issues. Such decisions are illustrated in many landmark cases.

5.1   Defamation cases

The Sketch Publishing Co & Anor vs Ajagbemokeferi(1989): A renowned Islamic preacher was conferred with the chieftaincy title Otun Balogun Oniwasu (meaning: second in rank to the general of Islamic preachers). Sketch published a 1979 almanac titled 'Voice of Islam', containing photographs of eminent Muslim leaders in Nigeria, including this particular preacher, Ajagbemokeferi. Under his photograph were inserted words in the Yoruba language which translate into: 'The second in rank to the General of Muslim preachers is a worthless and valueless chieftaincy just like chieftaincy titles of impostors and contrary to the tenets and teaching of Islam.'

Ajagbemokeferi went to the High Court, complaining of injury to his character and reputation. The court agreed that an ordinary person would regard the words in the circumstances as being capable of defamatory meaning but dismissed the action on the ground of the defence of fair comment.

The cleric appealed. The Court of Appeal found in his favour. *Sketch* appealed to the Supreme Court and won.

The Supreme Court judgment delivered by Justice Wali said:

> ... reading the whole words in the context and circumstances they were used, it is my view that they are not defamatory ... The evidence shows that from the time the words were allegedly published of and concerning the Respondent, he was not avoided or shunned. Nor did the evidence show that his status was lowered in the estimation of right-thinking men of his community or that he was exposed to hatred,

contempt or ridicule. There is no reliable evidence showing that the imputation on him is injurious to him in his office, profession, trade or business. He is still being respected as a prominent and respectful Islamic preacher by his local community. This is evidenced by his retention to continue with his weekly Friday sermon.[27]

Concord Press (Nig) Ltd vs Odutola: A case of plagiarism was made against a university don, against whom the University Council took action. The *Weekend Concord* published the story and Odutola went to court claiming N 15 million damages for libel. Concord Press put up defences of justification, qualified privilege and fair comment. The court decided in Odutola's favour and awarded him N 10 million. Concord Press took the case to the Appeal Court and won. The court found, among others:

(a) that a man cannot succeed in libel action where he has no reputation to protect;
(b) that Concord Press successfully pleaded justification, which it held is a complete defence in an action for libel.

5.2 Sedition cases

Director of Public Prosecutions vs Chike Obi (1961): Dr Chike Obi, a mathematician and social critic, was charged with sedition for distributing a pamphlet which attacked corrupt politicians. In the pamphlet, he had stated:

> Down with the enemies of the people, the exploiters of the weak and oppressors of the poor ... the days of those who have enriched themselves at the expense of the poor are numbered. The common man in Nigeria can today no longer be fooled by sweet talk at election time, only to be exploited and treated like dirt after the booty of office has been shared among the politicians.[28]

Despite the argument of Obi's counsel that sections 50 and 51 of the Criminal Code were inconsistent with section 24 (on freedom of expression) of the Constitution, and that it was not a law which is reasonably justifiable in a democratic society, the High Court found Obi guilty of sedition. However, it referred the case to the Supreme Court for proper interpretation of section 50 and 51 of the Criminal Code vis-à-vis section 24 of the 1960 Constitution of Nigeria. The Court said:

---

27 (1989) 1 Nigerian Weekly Law Reports (part 100) p. 696.
28 See R. Akinnola, 'Sedition', in R. Akinnola (ed.), *Nigerian Media and Legal Constraints*, Lagos: Centre for Free Speech, 1998, p. 182.

A person has a right to discuss any grievance, or criticize, canvass or censure acts of government and their public policy. He may even do this with a view to effecting a change in the party in power ... What is not permitted is to criticize the government in such a malignant manner for such attacks by their very nature tend to affect the public peace.[29]

Arthur Nwankwo vs State (1985):[30] In his book *How Jim Nwobodo Rules Anambra State*, published in 1982, Chief Nwankwo accused Chief Nwobodo, the state governor, of corruption and tyranny. The author was found guilty of sedition and sentenced to imprisonment of 12 months.

However, the Court of Appeal ruled that the law of sedition encapsulated in sections 50 and 51 of the Criminal Code was inconsistent with section 36 of the 1979 Constitution which guaranteed freedom of expression.

Justice Olatawura found:

It is my view that the law of sedition which has derogated from the freedom of speech guaranteed under this constitution is inconsistent with the 1979 constitution, more so when this cannot lead to a public disorder as envisaged under Section 41(a) of the 1979 constitution. We are no longer the illiterates or the mob society our colonial masters had in mind when the law was promulgated. The safeguard provided under Section 50(2) is inadequate, more so where the truth of what is published is no defence. To retain Section 51 of the Criminal Code in its present form, that is even if not inconsistent with the freedom of expression guaranteed by our constitution, will be a deadly weapon and to be used at will by a corrupt government or tyrant ... let us not diminish from the freedom gained from our colonial masters by resorting to laws enacted by them to suit their purpose. The decision of the founding fathers of this present constitution which guarantees freedom of speech which must include freedom to criticize should be praised and any attempt to derogate from it except as provided by the constitution must be resisted. Those in public office should not be intolerant of criticism. Where a writer exceeds the bounds, there should be a resort to the law of libel where the plaintiff must of necessity put his character and reputation in issue. Criticism is indispensable in a free society.[31]

---

29 (1961) 1 All Nigerian Law Reports p.194. Cited in Y. Osinbajo and K. Fogarn, *Nigerian Media Law*, Lagos: Gravitas Publishments, 1991, pp. 111–112.
30 (1985) 6 Nigerian Constitutional Law Reports p. 228.
31 See R. Akinnola, op cit., p. 184.

5.3   Cases on disclosure of news sources

Innocent Adikwu & Others vs Federal House of Representatives (1982):[32] The editor and journalists of the *Sunday Punch* newspaper were summoned by a committee of the House of Representatives, which demanded that they disclose the sources of an article. The journalists went to the High Court, claiming that the action of the House amounted to interference with their rights under section 36 of the 1979 Constitution. The court said:

> ... the newspapers are agents so to speak of the public to collect information which it is in the public interest to make known, and to feed the public of it. In support of this constitutional right of press freedom the newspaper cannot be required to disclose its sources of information except in grave or exceptional circumstances, neither by means of discovery before trial nor by questions or cross-examination at the trial. Nor by means of subpoenas from courts or summons by a legislative investigating body. The reason is because if newsmen were compelled to disclose their sources of information which it is not in the public interest to make known, charlatans would not be exposed, unfairness would go unremedied. Misdeeds and serious faults in the corridors of power and elsewhere would never be made known to the public.[33]

The case did not go on appeal.

Olusola Oyegbemi vs Attorney-General of the Federation (1982):[34] Reacting to a story in the *Daily Sketch* newspaper, police arrested the editor and a senior reporter and demanded the name of the source. When they refused, the police charged them with 'conspiracy to commit felony to wit: "false report"'. The journalists brought an application to the Lagos High Court for the enforcement of their fundamental human rights under the 1979 constitution. They claimed that the press could not be compelled to disclose its sources of information.

The court said:

> No person be he an Editor, Reporter or Publisher of a Newspaper can be compelled to disclose his source of information on any matter published by that person and non-disclosure cannot amount to contempt.

---

32 (1982) 3 Nigerian Constitutional Law Reports p. 394.
33 Ibid. note 34 at p. 412, cited in Osinbajo and Fogarn, op.cit., p.65.
34 (1982) 3 Nigerian Constitutional Law Reports p. 895.

But the court qualified this decision:

> However, this fundamental right is subject to the interest of justice, national
> security, public safety, public order, public morality, welfare of persons or prevention
> of disorder or crime. Consequently, the right to withhold information is not
> absolute.[35]

The Senate vs Tony Momoh (1983)[36]: The *Daily Times* published an article titled 'MPs,
Senators and Cards', on how senators lobbied for contracts from the executive arm
of government. The Senate summoned the editor to appear before it and disclose
the source of the information. The editor challenged the summons in court on the
ground that it infringed on his right of freedom of expression guaranteed in section
36 of the Constitution. He won in the High Court but the Senate appealed. The Court
of Appeal, without reversing the editor's victory at the High Court (he was not forced
to disclose the source), stated that there is nothing in section 36 of the Constitution
which contemplates any separate treatment of the news media or which confers any
express or implied right on a pressman not to disclose the source of his information
if he is required to do so.[37]

6   Conclusions and recommendations

Legislation and regulations constricting media freedom and freedom of expression
which date from colonial times have been used extensively by government authorities
since then and throughout the period of post-independence governance under military
and civilian rulers. Fifty years after political independence, such legislation remains
on the statute books and new laws are being enacted which retain the culture of
harshness.

Many of these laws are in contravention of the Declaration of Principles on
Freedom of Expression, which provides for the right of freedom of expression and
information.

---

35   Cited in M. Ozekhome, 'The Offensive Publications (Proscription) Decree no. 35 of 1993' , in Akinnola, op cit., p. 117.
36   (1983) 4 Nigerian Constitutional Law Reports p. 269.
37   ibid., p. 296–298. Cited in Osinbajo and Fogarn, p. 65.

Recommendations

- The following pieces of legislation should be repealed in their entirety:
    - The Nigerian Press Council Act;
    - Legislation on sedition – sections 50–52 of the Criminal Code and section 416 of the Penal Code;
    - Legislation on criminal defamation – sections 373–379 of the Criminal Code and sections 391–395 of the Penal Code;
    - The Official Secrets Act;
    - The Offensive Publications Decree 35 of 1993;
    - The Printing Presses Regulation Act;
    - The Newspaper Act and Newspaper Amendment Act.
- Laws to regulate the media should respect the principles of international human rights standards, including the International Covenant on Civil and Political Rights (ICCPR), African Charter on Human and Peoples' Rights and the Declaration of Principles on Freedom of Expression in Africa.
- The Freedom of Information Bill currently before the National Assembly should be passed into law only after a process of full public consultation to make sure that the final legislation is agreed to by civil society and other stakeholders. The Act should ensure that, among other things, access to information is granted by the state body in possession of the information sought, and that courts of law serve only as appeal mechanisms.
- An independent Press Council should be established to promote media self-regulation, enhance professional journalistic standards and serve as a complaints body for the public.

3
The Broadcasting Landscape

1   The state broadcasters

State/public broadcasters exist at two levels: those owned by the federal government and by the state (second tier) governments respectively. At the federal level are the Federal Radio Corporation of Nigeria (FRCN) and the Nigerian Television Authority (NTA). There is also the Voice of Nigeria (VON), which is the country's international radio broadcaster.

The FRCN operates a network of 37 channels, each with its own programming: a station headquarters in Abuja, four national stations located in Lagos, Kaduna, Enugu and Ibadan, and 32 others created over the past six years and based in the various states. The state governments own and run a combined 39 radio stations.

The FRCN is obliged by law to provide national coverage. The state (regional) government stations cover their respective territories, although the signals of some can be received in neighbouring states.

Credible audience reach and market share figures are hard to come by. But it is clear that the licensing of more commercial stations since 2003 has raised competition for listenership and market share.

Because of its national network and the obligatory link-up of state-owned stations to its national news programming, the FRCN enjoys the widest reach, but this does not appear to translate into listenership share in many areas of the country.

Data recorded in a 2007[38] report ranked the leading stations in audience share as follows:

---

38   Mediafacts – Nigeria/West Africa, MediaReachOMD Nigeria, 2007, pp. 33–34.

- Lagos: Raypower FM (private) – 23%; Radio Lagos – Tiwan Tiwan – 20%; Star FM (private) – 16%
- South East: Benue Radio FM, Markudi[39] – 25%; Cosmo FM (private), Enugu – 20%; Heartland FM, Owerri – 12%
- South West: Living Spring FM, Osogbo – 17%; BCOS FM, Ibadan – 14%; Positive FM, Akure – 13%; OSBC FM, Osogbo – 13%
- South South: AKBC FM – 37%; CR Radio FM, Calabar – 22%; Radio Nigeria, Port Harcourt – 15%
- North West: Freedom Radio (private), Kano – 28%; BBC Hausa Service – 20%; Radio Jigawa –12%
- North Central: FM 94, Lokoja – 13%; FM Minna – 11%; Zuma FM (private) – 9%
- North East: BBC Hausa Service – 18%; GSBC, Gombe –15%; ABC 1, Yola – 12%.

Apart from the Lagos and North West regions, state radio is still dominant in the country.

Ownership of television stations reflects the pattern in the radio sector. A network run by the federal government, the Nigerian Television Authority (NTA), has one national channel and 110 other stations (89 of them functioning). They are located in the various states and Abuja, the federal capital, and have their own programming but also links to network programming. Eight of these stations are designated Zonal Network Centres. A Zonal Network Centre is a station which coordinates operations of a number of other stations and through which network programmes for its zone are linked to the national network programming of the Authority.

The second tier of government, the states, along with the administration of the federal capital territory, control 37 stations.

Television viewership shares according to the 2007 report[40] are as follows:

- Lagos: Silverbird Television (private) – 29%; AIT (private) – 28%; Galaxy TV (private) – 16%
- South East: NTA Markudi[41] – 11%; NTA Enugu – 10%; RSTV Port Harcourt – 9%
- South West: NTA Ibadan – 14%; BCOS Ibadan – 14%; OSRC Akure – 13%
- South South: NTA Uyo – 15%; RSTV Port Harcourt – 12%; AKBC Uyo – 12%
- North West: AIT Kano (private) – 14%; NTA Kano – 13%; NTA Kastina – 12%

39 The station is located in the north central zone. The fact that it has an audience share in the neighbouring south east zone is due to a spill–over of its signals to this area.
40 Ibid., pp. 29–30.
41 See footnote 39.

- North Central: NTA Minna – 17%; NTA Lokoja – 12%; NTA Ilorin – 10%.

Outside Lagos, state television is still dominant.

2   Commercial/private broadcasters

The 60-year government monopoly on the broadcast sector was broken in 1992 with the promulgation of the National Broadcasting Commission (NBC) Decree no. 38. Among other things, the law provided for a regulatory body and private participation in ownership and operation in the broadcasting industry. The NBC, as stipulated in the law, began to 'receive, process and consider applications for ownership of radio and television stations, including cable television services, direct satellite broadcast and any other medium of broadcasting' in 1993.

Between 1993 and 2001, a total of nine television, eight radio, two global satellite television and 15 satellite re-transmission stations were licensed. In 2002, a further 16 radio and five television licences were granted. The latest batch of licence approvals for 28 radio and ten television stations was announced in February 2007. Seventeen private stations now operate in the radio category, 14 in television and 38 in pay-TV.

The government says it is committed to enhancing diversity in the sector to achieve goals which include democracy-building. Announcing the 2002 set of licences, information minister Prof. Jerry Gana said that 'this administration in issuing these licences is demonstrating its firm belief that only an enlightened citizenry can sustain democracy'.[42]

His successor, Frank Nweke Jnr, also told industry stakeholders in July 2006 that 'the government appreciated the importance of a plural and diverse media landscape in the expansion of the country's democratic space'.[43]

However, several regulatory decisions and actions of the NBC have sparked controversy and elicited criticism from commercial operators, leading many practitioners and industry watchers to conclude that a huge gap still exists between government's proclaimed goal of promoting diversity and the reality on the ground.

The most contentious issue is that of the fees private operators are being charged. The law empowers the NBC to charge fees and levies. According to section 13(1)(g) of the NBC Act, 'The commission shall have the power with respect to any licence granted under Section 9 of this Decree to prescribe an appropriate fee payable.'

---

42   'Government Grants 21 Broadcast Licences', *Media Rights Monitor*, March 2002, p. 4.
43   'Ministerial Support for Community Radio', *The Guardian*, 17 July 2006.

Commercial radio licences are in two categories: Category A, which applies to locations in Lagos, Port Harcourt and Abuja, attracts a fee of N 20 million (US$ 167 000) while category B, which is for all other locations countrywide, costs N 15 million (US$ 125 000). For television, the fees are N 15 million (US$ 125 000) and N 11.25 million (US$ 93 750) for categories A and B respectively.

A commercial licence has a five-year life span, and each renewal costs N 12.5 million (US$ 104 000) for Category A and N10 million (US$ 83 000) for Category B. In addition, each station is required to pay to NBC 2.5 per cent of its gross turnover as annual charges.

In contrast, government owned stations are required to pay a licence fee of N 5 million (US$ 41 666) only. They are not required to pay renewal fees or annual charges.

The commission justifies the licence fees disparity by arguing that 'a public station covers a state and is required to pay N 2.5 million for a five-year period [while] a private station that covers a minimum of four states pays a commercial licence fee of N 15 million for television and N 20 million for radio at the maximum'.[44]

The Independent Broadcasting Association of Nigeria (IBAN) suggests that the power to review fees should be vested in the national legislature rather than the NBC.

Private broadcasters also criticise the fact that the regulatory body does not allow for cost-saving networking arrangements among commercial stations, even in cases of collaboration with government-owned broadcasters. The commission says it does not have a legal instrument to authorise networking by any broadcast station except as granted by law to the Nigerian Television Authority (NTA) and the Federal Radio Corporation of Nigeria (FRCN).[45]

Entertainment dominates on commercial radio with little attention to news.

In television, competition is high in news and entertainment. Unsatisfied with the supply of soap operas from the prolific Nigerian home video industry, stations have turned to imported material from places like Latin America. For example, AIT and MITV air *El Cuepro Del Deseo* (Second Chance), a Mexican soap, at 21h00 to 22h00 and 19h00 to 20h00 respectively, from Monday to Friday. Silverbird TV shows *La Revancha* at 20h00 to 21h00 from Monday to Thursday.

Nigerian producers have to compete for space with such imported material and their lack of financial muscle often puts them at a distinct disadvantage. To have their production broadcast, producers have to pay the television companies for airtime. They recoup their investment from advertisements or sponsorships which they have to source themselves. Wale Adenuga, who produces at least four major soaps currently on television, says:

44 'NBC's reforms attract sharp reactions from industry operators', *Vanguard*, 7 April 2004, p. 27.
45 'The Law is our shepherd – NBC', *Media Rights Monitor*, September 2001, p. 7.

> The biggest destroyer of good TV programmes in Nigeria is the advent of Mexican soaps ... If you watch our TV stations 7pm and 9pm you see these Mexican soaps. And Nigerians are addicted to them, so there is no way a Nigerian programme scheduled for 10pm will compete with them ... 'Super Story', as acceptable as it is, can't get two days in a week on any station. But Mexican soap takes six days a week. I have enough money to pay, but they refused because the people bringing in the soaps have more money.[46]

Advocacy efforts from industry stakeholders in this regard appear to have yielded fruit. Early in 2009, the regulatory body, the NBC, directed broadcasting stations to move foreign soaps out of the family belt, that is, the time slot from 19h00 to 22h00. The direction took effect from April 2009 and stations have complied.

Despite being relative newcomers on the broadcasting scene, the commercial stations are acquiring appreciable audience shares. According to 2007 data,[47] Silverbird Television (29 per cent), AIT Lagos (28 per cent) and Galaxy TV Lagos (16 per cent) lead in the Lagos area; AIT Kano (14 per cent) tops the chart in the North West; while AIT Abuja (10 per cent) is fourth in North Central.

In radio, five stations (Raypower FM, Star FM, Brilla FM, Cool FM and Rhythm FM) together have 72 per cent of listenership in the Lagos area; Cosmo FM, Enugu, alone has 20 per cent in the South East, 10 per cent in the South-South and 25 per cent in the South West. Freedom Radio, Kano (28 per cent) is the leader in the North West, where Nagarta Radio, Kaduna (9 per cent) is also in the top-ten bracket. Zuma FM (9 per cent), Cool FM, Abuja (7 per cent) and Okin FM, Offa (6 per cent), occupy the third, fifth and seventh positions respectively in North Central.

Ownership of commercial stations comes from a diversity of backgrounds such as journalism, business and politics.

In some cases, the ownership background reflects in the station's orientation and programming. For example, Larry Izamoje was a sports journalist for many years and his Brilla FM station offers all-sport programming. The Silverbird Group and the Murray-Bruces have been in the entertainment business for a long time. Silverbird TV focuses mainly on entertainment and even its news bulletins have special entertainment segments. Channels TV has a strong concentration on news. Its chief executive, John Momoh, comes from a background of news and current affairs programming at NTA, the state broadcaster.

---

46 'An utterance that made me change the former cast of Papa Ajasco – Wale Adenuga', *Saturday Punch*, 21 June 2008, pp. 48–49.
47 Mediafacts – 2007, op cit., pp. 29–30, 33–34.

Table 2:   Ownership background of major commercial broadcast stations

Name of station	Type	Identifiable owner	Background
Africa Independent Television	TV	Dr Raymond Dokpesi	Engineering/Business/Politics
Channels Television	TV	Mr John Momoh	Journalism/Broadcasting
Murhi International TV	TV	Alh. Muri Busari Gbadeyanka	Business
Minaj Broadcast Intl TV	TV	Senator Mike Ajegbo	Politics
Silverbird TV	TV	Ben Murray Bruce Guy Murray Bruce	Business/Entertainment Business/Entertainment
Galaxy TV	TV	Steve Ojo	Journalism/Broadcasting
Desmins Int. TV	TV	Khalifa Baba Ahmed	Journalism/Broadcasting
Raypower FM	Radio	Dr Raymond Dokpesi	Engineering/Business
Star FM	Radio	Alh. Muri Busari Gbadeyanka	Business
Freedom Radio	Radio	Alh. Bashir Dalhatu	Business
Brilla FM	Radio	Larry Izamoje	Journalism/Broadcasting
Cosmo FM	Radio	Dr Chimaroke Nnamani	Politics
Rhythm FM	Radio	Ben Murray-Bruce Guy Murray-Bruce	Business/Entertainment Business/Entertainment
Hot FM	Radio	Senator Chris Anyanwu	Journalism/Politics

Source: Research by author

3   Community broadcasting services

Existing law and policy have not given specific recognition to community broadcasting in Nigeria.

Section 9(1)(a) of the NBC Act 38 (as amended by Act 55 of 1999) says that an applicant for a broadcasting licence shall be 'a body corporate registered under the Companies and Allied Matters Decree 1990 or a station owned, established or operated by the Federal, State or Local Government'. But section 9(4) provides that the NBC shall consider 'the structure of shareholding in the broadcasting organization' and 'the number of shareholding in other media establishments' in determining the grant of a licence.

Community members who manage or participate in community broadcasting are not shareholders. And under Nigerian law, entities seeking non-profit incorporation are registered as a trusteeship with the Corporate Affairs Commission. The legal corporate document required for this purpose is the group's constitution.

The NBC has indicated its willingness to waive or modify these requirements, seemingly relying on its powers under the NBC Act, which gives the commission under section 2(a) the function of 'advising government on broadcasting policy implementation'. Section 2(p) also empowers it to carry out 'such other activities as are necessary or expedient for the full discharge of all or any of the functions conferred on it under or pursuant to this decree'.

The Commission has made provision for community broadcasting in its National Broadcasting Code, first in 2002 and with further elaboration in the current (2006) edition.

The Code describes community broadcasting as

> a key agent of democratization for social, cultural and economic development ... a non-profit, grassroots public broadcast service medium through which community members are able to contribute and foster civic responsibility and integration.

The Code lists the community corporate entities which could run broadcast stations as 'a local not-for-profit organization; an educational institution (campus); a cultural association; a cooperative society; and a partnership of associations'.

It disqualifies religious organisations, political parties, individuals, and profit-oriented corporate bodies from being granted community broadcast licences. In determining the sustainability of applications, the commission will consider, among other things, ownership, funding, the constitution of the board of trustees, and the nature and content of programming, particularly on political and religious matters, throughout the lifespan of the licence.[48]

Dissatisfied with the absence of rural community broadcasting and an enabling environment for its emergence, civil society groups started an advocacy process in 2003. A local organisation, the Institute for Media and Society, along with the Panos Institute West Africa (PIWA) and the World Association of Community Radio Broadcasters (AMARC) launched an 'Initiative for Building Community Radio in Nigeria'.

Outcomes of the campaign include widespread awareness in critical constituencies such as grassroots groups, non-governmental organisations, media, academia, and international development agencies, as well as among government policy-makers, and legislative and regulatory bodies.

The federal government has responded through statements and the institution of policy processes. Three policy documents developed by the government are awaiting final pronouncements and release to the public. They are the reviewed National Mass Communication Policy, the National Community Radio Policy and the National Frequency Spectrum Management Policy. The draft review of the Mass

---

48   Nigeria Broadcasting Code (4th edition), 2006, pp. 72–74.

Communication Policy provides in its section 4(4) that 'there shall be an equitable spread of the categories of licence to ensure that no community or segment of the population is denied access to information through the electronic media' and that 'the development of community broadcasting shall be promoted'. The draft Community Radio Policy elaborates a framework for community radio development which deals with such issues as access, participation and ownership; licensing; programming content and language; governance and management; technical arrangements; sustainability and funding; research and capacity-building; and monitoring and evaluation.

These documents on broadcasting regulation and on-going policy reform efforts appear to have informed the granting of a radio broadcasting licence to the University of Lagos in 2002 and eight other institutions of higher learning in 2007. A campus radio station pays a licence fee of N 1 million (US$ 6 600) for a five-year period.

The University of Lagos station (Unilag FM) began official transmission in 2003. The station sees itself as the first university radio station as well as the first community radio station in Nigeria.[49]

Though located in the main campus of the University of Lagos within mainland Lagos, the station says its signals are received in neighbouring Ogun state. This is necessary because it has to reach the institution's several campuses and students of its Distance Learning Institute (DLI) located in many settlements, with specially designed educational programmes. According to 2007 data,[50] the station has a 2 per cent share of the listenership in the Lagos area.

The station generates its income from such sources as grants from donors and advertisements. Because of the station's status, the NBC is said to have been unfavourably disposed towards it running commercials in the initial stages. But the station's management insisted that 'there is nothing wrong for a community station to run a commercial advertisement ... "not-for-profit" does not mean "for loss". The type of commercials we put up here are those that are beneficial to our community'. They explained that although they are a small community station, they have a lot of overheads to take care of in the daily running of the operation.

Media experts observed that the programming of Unilag FM is not substantially different from that of commercial stations in the country. They claim that entertainment has become dominant. The station's management says that changes have been introduced to make the programming reflect the taste and needs of the university community.

---

49 'Unilag FM: First Community radio in Nigeria', interview with W.K Bello, pioneer coordinator of Unilag FM, in
    Airwaves, October-December 2006, pp. 13–15.
50 Mediafacts – 2007, op cit., p. 33.

Initially, the station operated under the supervision of the vice-chancellor's office. According to members of the management team they have not experienced any pressure or editorial interference from the institution's authorities or other influences.

Following a change in the university's leadership in mid-2007, the management of the station was transferred to the department of mass communication. This gives the supervision responsibility to the head of the department of mass communication and links the station's operation with practical training of mass communication students in the University.

Another set of 18 campus radio licences were issued in early 2009, for example, for the University of Ibadan, Federal University of Technology Minna, Nnamdi Azikiwe University Awka, Bayero University Kano, Babcock University Ilishan and Obafemi Awolowo University Ile-Ife.

4   Technical standard and accessibility of services

Stations of the major national radio broadcaster, the FRCN and those of the regional (state) broadcasters transmit on amplitude modulation (AM) or frequency modulation (FM) while private/commercial radio broadcasters use FM.

Except for a few government-controlled stations which are still on very high frequency (VHF), television operators have migrated to ultra high frequency (UHF).

Transmitter power at federal radio ranges from 20 to 25 KW for AM, and from 10 to 20 KW for FM stations. In the regions (states), transmitter power is between 10 and 50 KW for AM and between 10 and 30 KW for FM. Commercial stations operate with transmitters of between 5 and 10 KW. Most of the country is covered by the combined networks of government and commercial stations. Research data are not available to confirm proportion of coverage.

For television, transmitter power in government-controlled stations is between 10 and 100 KW, while commercial stations generally use slightly more powerful transmitters with a 30 to 145 KW capacity.

Availability of electricity is erratic in both urban and rural areas of the country. The poor state of power supply has not improved significantly since 1999 for household and commercial consumers. Nigeria's electricity sector, long dominated by a state monopoly, the National Electric Power Authority (now the Power Holding Company of Nigeria), provides less than 4 000 megawatts to the country, although total national demand is put at 7 000 megawatts.[51] Broadcasting organisations have to invest in the purchase

---

51   Dr Ransome Owan, chair, National Electricity Regulatory Commission (NERC), interview in *ThisDay*, 22 July 2008, p. 38.

and maintenance of private electric generators to power their operations, in some cases for up to 24 hours daily. This also implies that a large proportion of potential radio and television audiences are denied access because they do not have alternative sources to power their sets.

Post-independence broadcast media development activities did not pay attention to concerted acquisition or standardisation of equipment, particularly in the absence of local manufacture or assembly of equipment.

Organisations purchased equipment from different foreign manufacturers, leading to numerous types and models being used, often incompatible with each other. In addition, equipment was not regularly renewed to keep pace with changing technologies, and appropriate investments were not made to acquire additional equipment necessary for expanding operations.

As a result, equipment in broadcasting houses, especially the state-owned ones, is often obsolete and inadequate. It is still common to find analogue equipment only gradually being replaced by digital systems. Access of personnel to computers and allied technologies is still low in many places; reporters have to queue for the few available cameras in many TV stations, meaning that coverage of events and issues is often hampered. The commercial stations have more technologically advanced equipment than the government-owned stations.

5   Concentration of media ownership

Important information on ownership in the broadcast sector is shrouded in excessive secrecy particularly during the licensing process. The use of proxies by many investors in this sector does not help matters.

Nevertheless, there is some legislative provision for control of cross-ownership. Section 9(4)(a) and (b) of NBC Act 38 says that in determining the granting of a licence, the NBC shall consider 'the structure of shareholding in the broadcasting organization' and 'the number of shareholding in other media establishments'. Section 9(5) also provides that it 'shall be illegal for any person to have controlling shares in more than two television stations'.

Section 4(b) of the NBC (Amendment) Act 55 has changed this to read more specifically: 'It shall be illegal for any person to have controlling shares in more than two of each of the broadcast sectors of transmission'.

6 Conclusions and recommendations

Nigeria's liberalisation journey in the broadcasting sector has gone only halfway, concentrating almost exclusively on commercial broadcasting. This is not in line with both the letter and spirit of the Declaration of Principles on Freedom of Expression in Africa which provide for the encouragement of a diverse, independent broadcasting sector, including the promotion of community broadcasting.

Recommendations

- The government should complete all the policy processes it initiated – regarding a National Mass Communication Policy, National Frequency Management Policy, and National Community Radio Policy – and embark on legal reform. It should work in consultation with advocacy groups to ensure that the draft policies comply with accepted international democratic standards.
- Industry stakeholders, including the regulatory agency, should address the issue of possible cooperative management of transmission and standardisation of equipment. This is particularly important now in the era of digitalisation, with different technologies offered by developed countries.
- The NBC should begin to license rural, suburban and urban community broadcasting stations, including campus radios.
- Licence fees for commercial broadcasters should be reduced while community broadcasters should get their licences for free or a nominal amount. Annual charges should be suspended until an independent regulator is in place, the economic/business environment of broadcasting improves, and stakeholders agree on the amount to be charged.
- To prevent concentration in the media industry, one person or body should not be allowed to have controlling shares in more than one radio and one TV station simultaneously.
- The NBC, training/research and other institutions should conduct studies on such subjects as technical coverage of the country, and audience research.
- Technical quality standards should be reinforced and more widely adopted.

4
Digitalisation and its Impact

The International Telecommunications Union (ITU), a United Nations agency tasked with coordinating global telecommunications and services, has set a deadline of 17 June 2015 for broadcasters in Europe, Africa, the Middle East and the Islamic Republic of Iran to migrate to digital television broadcasting technology, on both the transmission and the reception side. The ITU deadline refers only to the digitalisation of television broadcasting. Deadlines for the digitalisation of radio have not yet been determined.

The ITU-agreement, however, allows for an additional five years up to 2020 for many African countries, among them Nigeria, beyond the 2015 cut-off point,[52] even though some have voluntarily committed themselves to the earlier deadline.

The ITU sees the digitalisation of broadcasting as a means of establishing a more equitable, just and people-centred information society, leapfrogging 'existing technologies to connect the unconnected in underserved and remote communities and close the digital divide'.[53]

The switch-over from analogue to digital broadcasting will expand the potential for a greater convergence of services, with digital terrestrial broadcasting supporting mobile reception of video, internet and multimedia data. Digitalisation of television is seen as a means of enhancing the viewer's experience by enabling better quality viewing through wide-screen, high definition pictures and surround sound, as well as interactive services. It also allows for innovations such as handheld TV broadcasting devices (Digital Video Broadcasting-Handheld, or DVB-H), and will mean greater bandwidth for telecommunication services.[54] Importantly, it will also allow for the creation of many more television and radio channels through greater spectrum efficiency.

---

52 'Digital broadcasting set to transform the communication landscape by 2015', June 2006, http://www.itu.int/newsroom/press_releases/2006/11.html.
53 Ibid.
54 Ibid.

1   Preparedness for the switch-over

The process of digitalisation in the broadcasting industry began in 2007 when the government approved December 2007 as the start-off date for the transition from analogue to digital broadcasting. The regulatory body, the National Broadcasting Commission (NBC), ordered all pay-TV operations to switch over by the end of that year and started to enforce this deadline when it shut down analogue cable TV stations on 1 January 2008. The stations were later granted a reprieve and a new switch-over date was set for 31 March 2008. The NBC announced in June 2008 that a 90 per cent switch-over rate had been attained, and that the small number of operators who had not yet switched over were likely to be in the process of clearing their imported equipment with the customs authorities.[55]

Government set up a 27-member presidential advisory committee on digitalisation in September 2008 which submitted its report in June 2009 to the minister of information and communication, Prof. Dora Akunyili, on behalf of the president. While the report is not yet in the public domain, the committee gave an insight into some of its recommendations when presenting the document during a press conference. These recommendations include, among others, the separation of the functions of broadcast content providers and signal distributors with the consequent introduction of two categories of licences: broadcasting content licences and broadcasting signal distribution licences. At the time of writing, government had not announced its position on the recommendations.

Broadcasters generally appreciate the inevitability of the digital migration and investments are being made into the purchase of the necessary hardware, with all digital equipment having to be imported at high cost. According to the NBC, over 90 per cent digitalisation in production and post-production equipment has been achieved nationwide.[56]

In addition, many stations are giving attention to the appropriate skilling of their workforce – through training of existing staff and insisting that newly recruited members possess the requisite information technology skills.

The potential economic cost of digitalisation to the Nigerian consumer is cause for concern for stakeholders, including the government. It is feared that many citizens will not be able to afford the set-top boxes required to receive digital TV signals, which come at a cost of more than US$ 110 per box. In total, an estimated US$ 2.7 billion

---

55   'Nigeria attains 90% digitalization in cable broadcasting', *The Punch*, 17 June 2008, p. 8.
56   'Government and people must work together to reduce digitalization cost – NBC Boss', *Vanguard*, 2 July 2008.

will be needed for the purchase of set-top boxes for 24 million TV sets nationwide, according to the NBC.[57]

The government has acknowledged this challenge. Former information minister, Frank Nweke Jnr, told a 2006 international conference of African stakeholders in Abuja, the Nigerian capital:

> We [government] strongly desire media penetration to larger sections of our populations, but we are now faced with the prospect of a reversal occasioned by possible inability of large numbers to upgrade receivers or acquire new sets due to their economic circumstances.[58]

The advisory committee therefore recommended a policy to make the new technology more accessible and affordable to the general public through the set-top box. Experts have suggested that the government should ease the financial burden on consumers through such measures as provision of free or subsidised set-top boxes.

2   Convergence

Mobile phones can now be used for the reception of radio and television. Many brands of handsets (mobile phone receivers) are easily configured to receive signals from various radio stations in the country.

In August 2007, MultiChoice, a company which operates the Digital Satellite Television (DSTV) platform, introduced Digital Video Broadcasting – Handheld, DVB-H, a technological standard which allows digital broadcasting of television and audio feed to a mobile phone. The service was launched through an affiliate company, Details Nigeria, which concluded its first distribution agreement with MTN Nigeria, a local mobile phone operator.

Similar arrangements have also been initiated by mobile phone operators, following their acquisition of Third Generation (3G) licences in late 2006. For example, Globacom, a major operator, announced plans to introduce Triple Play, a service that offers high-speed internet, television and telephone. It recently launched a facility which makes the signal of Silverbird TV, a local channel, available to its subscribers.

On many stations the audience can take part in competitions and game shows and make requests on live television broadcasts through short messaging services (sms)

---

57   'Nigerians to pay $2.7 billion for digital broadcasting', *The Punch*, 24 June 2008, p. 24.
58   'Govt to attain full digital technology by 2015', *The Guardian*, 24 May 2006.

from mobile phones. It is common to find interactive sms messages being scrolled on TV screens in between news updates and adverts.

The regulatory body, NBC, sees these services as adding value to telephony and considers their operations satisfactory as long as the content provider is licensed and the content conforms to the provisions of the Nigeria Broadcasting Code.

3   Increased competition

The broadcasting industry expects an explosion in the number of players in addition to the 406 licencees now in existence. The resulting competition will be even fiercer in a business environment which is said to be tough already.

4   Conclusion and recommendations

A prime source of concern is whether Nigeria will meet the 2015 deadline set by the ITU. The delay in policy development and implementation gives the impression that there is insufficient political will and commitment by government. This is all the more concerning because the work can only proceed once the policy framework is in place.

Recommendations

- The government should speedily translate the report of the presidential advisory committee on digitalisation into public policy, organise public consultations, invite public input, issue its white paper and give implementation directives.
- The existing broadcasting law and regulation should be reviewed to incorporate issues of broadcasting digitalisation.
- The National Population Commission should release data gathered on TV/radio-set ownership from the last population and household census, so that this information will be available for broadcasting policies and planning.
- The NBC should be empowered to conduct surveys and update the data gathered on TV/radio-set ownership during the last census.
- The NBC should continue to create awareness about the importance and challenges of digitalisation.

5
Broadcasting Legislation and Regulation

1   The National Broadcasting Commission

Broadcasting regulation is the responsibility of the National Broadcasting Commission (NBC). The commission was created by a military law, the National Broadcasting Commission Decree 38 of 1992. When Nigeria returned to civil, constitutional government in 1999 the decree (along with its 1999 amendment) became an Act of Parliament. Hence it is now called the National Broadcasting Commission Act, although the term 'decree' remains in the texts of the principal and subsidiary laws.

The law terminated government's monopoly of broadcasting and opened the door for private participation through ownership and operation in the sector. However, it gives the Commission limited regulatory independence and subordinates it to government executive bodies, namely the ministry of information and the presidency.

Section 2(1) of the Act provides for the Commission to carry out a wide array of functions: advising the federal government on policy implementation on broadcasting; processing and recommending broadcasting licence applications to the president through the information minister; undertaking research and development; establishing an industry code and setting standards; addressing public complaints; upholding equity and fairness; promoting indigenous cultures and community life; measuring audiences and penetration levels; harmonising government policies on trans-border transmission and reception; monitoring for harmful emission, interference and illegal broadcasting; determining and applying sanctions; approving transmitter power, station's location, coverage areas and equipment types; and carrying out other activities necessary for the discharge of its functions.

The subsidiary (also military-made) legislation, NBC (Amendment) Decree (now Act) 55 of 1999, added the following functions: ensuring manpower development through broadcast curricula and programme accreditation; arbitration in industry conflicts; ensuring adherence to laws, rules and regulation on foreign and local capital participation in broadcasting; serving as national legislative and regulatory consultants on broadcasting issues (that is, being the agency of reference for advice to government on broadcasting matters); and guaranteeing and ensuring the liberty and protection of the industry with due respect to the law.

Section 2(1)(b) and (c) of the principal Act (Decree 38 of 1992) restricts the NBC's role in the licensing process to 'receiving, processing and considering applications' and 'recommending applications through the Minister to the President, Commander-in-Chief of the Armed Forces for the grant of radio licences'. The final authority for the granting of licences rests with the president. This is in line with section 39(2) of the Constitution which empowers the president (and not an independent regulator) to license broadcasters:

> Provided that no person, other than the government of the Federation or of a state or any other person or body authorized by the President on the fulfillment of conditions laid down by an act of the National Assembly, shall own, establish or operate a television or wireless broadcasting station for any purpose whatsoever.

Under the NBC Act, various superintending powers over the commission are given to the information minister:

- Section 6 empowers the minister to give 'directives of a general character' to the commission, and 'it shall be the duty of the commission to comply with such directives'.
- Should the NBC decide to borrow funds, section 17 stipulates that the minister's consent must be obtained.
- According to section 19, the NBC must prepare and submit its annual report, including audited accounts, to the minister.
- According to section 20, the making of regulations by the NBC for the purpose of giving effect to the provisions of the Act must receive the minister's approval.

The Act (as amended) provides for a decision-making body of the NBC which comprises a chairman, ten other members and the director-general. The ten members are to represent the following interests: law, business, culture, education, social science, broadcasting, public affairs, engineering, state security services and the federal ministry of information and culture. The last two interests were included in the amendment law presumably to strengthen government's presence in the NBC.

The members of the NBC, including the chairman and the director-general, are all appointed by the president on the recommendation of the information minister. This is at the discretion of the minister and there is no public participation in the process.

As is the case with appointments, the president has power to remove any member of the commission 'if he is satisfied that it is not in the interest of the commission or in the interest of the public that the member should continue in office'. This has not happened yet but it could, given that it has a legal basis. The government alone defines 'interest of the commission' and 'interest of the public'.

These provisions have the combined effect of denying the regulatory body full regulatory powers and institutional independence and creating arbitrariness in the regulatory process. Specific concerns include the following:

- With the latitude given to the president, he or she could easily appoint a commission dominated by government officials and/or members of the ruling party.
- The inclusion of the representatives of the federal ministry of information and the state security service will enhance government's ability to intimidate and control the NBC's decision-making process.
- The absence of provisions in the law regarding the process by which constituencies ought to be represented and to make inputs into appointments does not make for transparency.
- The absence of clearly defined security of tenure for the director-general and members of the commission might expose them to political pressure to act in accordance with the wishes of the minister or president.

For several years after the promulgation of NBC Act 38, state broadcasters did not want to submit to the regulatory powers of the NBC, arguing that they predated the NBC and that there was no express provision in the law putting them under the Commission's purview. For this reason, the 1999 Amendment Act clarified that '[a]ny broadcast station transmitting in Nigeria before the commencement of the Decree shall be deemed to have been licensed under this Decree and, accordingly, shall be subject to the provisions of this Decree'.

While the regulatory activities of the NBC have now been extended to cover the state broadcasters, there are still signs of the old times. The Nigerian Television Authority (NTA) and the Federal Radio Corporation of Nigeria (FRCN) began expansion programmes in 2000, involving the establishment of more stations across the country. Government approved the programme. The NBC played no part in either the approval or implementation processes.

The NBC has a mixed strategy on the involvement of the public or stakeholders in its regulatory operations. The Commission organises public fora, seminars, conferences and retreats through which it brings together operators and members of the public to discuss issues affecting the industry. Matters covered at these event depend on participants' priorities. For example, at a 2005 public forum the dominant issues were: imitation of foreign accents by English language presenters; upsurge of religious programmes with unverifiable claims; unprofessional transmission of offensive scenes such as fatal accidents; poor technical transmission of programmes by cable stations; excessive transmission of programmes which stereotype women as witches; and excessive showing of ritual killings. The forum also criticised the NBC for being hard on private stations while showing leniency towards government ones.[59] One of the outcomes of these consultations is the Nigeria Broadcasting Code, the industry regulatory document which the NBC reviews and publishes every three years.

A structured broadcasting policy framework does not exist as a basis for the work of the NBC. The only existing policy document, the National Mass Communication Policy of 1990, expressly said 'the time is not yet ripe for private ownership of the electronic media'. The 1992 NBC Act reversed this position, but a new policy has not been produced.

In response to stakeholders' advocacy, government began a review of the 1990 policy in mid-2004 and started the process of developing a new National Community Radio Policy as well as a National Frequency Management Policy in 2006.

Working Groups on the 1990 policy and the community radio policy submitted reports to government which in turn asked the public to make their inputs. The Working Group on Frequency Management Policy invited and received memoranda from the public, but nothing more has since been heard about its work. The government has yet to issue final documents to the public from all three exercises.

2   Licensing of broadcasters and enforcement of licence conditions

The NBC receives, collates and processes applications for broadcasting licences and forwards them with their recommendation to the Information Minister, who in turn submits his recommendation to the President for his consideration.

Each applicant has to complete an application form to be purchased from the NBC at a cost of N 50 000 (US$ 424) and provide, among others, a feasibility study including the engineering design of the proposed station as well as an undertaking

---

59   *Open Forum in Port Harcourt*, NBC News, Oct–Dec 2005, p. 12; *Resolutions*, NBC News, July–Sept 2005, p. 12 and *Communique*, NBC News, April–June 2006, p. 12.

that the station will be used to promote national interest, unity and cohesion. It must also undertake not to offend religious sensibilities or promote ethnicity, sectionalism, hatred and disaffection among the peoples of Nigeria. While the latter obligation seems to be reasonable, it is questionable whether stations can and should be obliged to promote 'national interest, unity and cohesion', with the definition of what that is supposed to mean known only to the regulatory agency.

The NBC processes and forwards the application to the minister of information and onwards to the president who gives final approval at his discretion. This process is shrouded in secrecy and has no fixed time frame. Each stage – NBC, minister and presidency – works at its own speed. Consequently, applicants often wait for years without getting results and the regulatory body is not obliged to offer any explanation.

Public hearings have been held in some exceptional cases of licence renewal, particularly concerning broadcasters around whom controversy had developed. An example is Multichoice. A prominent operator in the pay-TV sector, the company was criticised for, among other things, high tariffs, airing of materials classified as NTBB (not to be broadcast) by the regulator, and laxity in education programming. The issues were discussed at a May 2004 public hearing. The company's licence was then renewed by the NBC.

Licensing of a broadcaster 'shall be subject to availability of broadcast frequencies' (Section 9[2] of the NBC Act). The NBC takes bulk broadcasting sector allocation of frequencies from the National Frequency Management Council, keeps custody of the data and solely determines availability. The public has no access to this information and the regulatory body could use it to reject applications. Section 9(3) also provides that: 'Compliance with the requirements specified in sub-section (1) of this section shall not entitle an applicant to the grant of a licence but the grant of a licence by the commission shall not be unreasonably withheld.' There is no provision for appeal if a licence is withheld and unsuccessful applicants have not been going to court to seek redress.

According to the third schedule of the NBC Act (as amended), a broadcasting licence is valid for five years in the first instance and a renewal is required if a licensee wants to continue operating her/his station. The commission may refuse to renew a licence if after considering past performance of the station it is not in the 'national or public interest' or in the interest of the broadcast industry to do so. Again, the national or public interest or that of the broadcast industry are not clearly defined. They are what the NBC might arbitrarily determine them to be.

Majority shares in a broadcasting company must be held by Nigerians. 'Majority shares' are not precisely quantified but former information minister Jerry Gana gave insight into government's reasoning on this issue when in May 2001 he asked the NBC to properly scrutinise proposals by foreign media interested in investing in the nation's broadcast industry so as to save the country from being taken over by foreign investors. He said: 'Our airwaves shall be considered sacrosanct and it shall only serve great and noble causes of Nigerian people and media practitioners. I consider it rather obnoxious to fight off one form of colonialism only to replace it with another form from the back door.'[60]

In April 2004 the NBC forbade the relay of live news and news programmes of foreign stations. It argued that the basis of its ban on the relay of foreign news is contained in section 5 of the Broadcasting Code which states:

> A terrestrial free-to-air station shall not relay foreign news content 'live' ... shall not relay foreign news content in its entirety, even delayed ... (but these provisions) do not preclude the universal practice of using excerpts for news; in which circumstances, the local station assumes editorial responsibility.

The third schedule of the NBC Act (as amended) prescribes that programme content for a radio or television station shall be at least 60 per cent local and not more than 40 per cent foreign. The Nigeria Broadcasting Code, on the other hand, sets local content at a minimum of 70 per cent. The reason for this inconsistency is not known. For cable or subscription stations, local content should not be less than 20 per cent. All these content ratios were arbitrarily fixed without any industry or public consultations.

Section 10 of the NBC Act disqualifies religious organisations and political parties from being granted a licence. The reasons are not stated in the law but the provision may have been informed by the occurrence of numerous religious–induced conflicts in many parts of the country, the bitterness with which party-political contests are conducted, and the possible fear that putting broadcasting stations in the hands of these two groups might just amount to licensing them to destroy the country.

The exclusion of religious groups in particular has not been without criticism. It has been argued that despite the incidence of religious fundamentalism and conflicts in the country's history, the need for pluralism is strong enough to compel a rethink of this provision. A case-by-case approach is suggested in place of a blanket ban.[61]

---

60 NBC Dialogue with broadcast executives, *Media Rights Monitor*, May 2001, p. 11.
61 See, for example, L. Uka Uche, 'The deregulation of Nigeria's broadcast industry in a global market economy', in: Uche (ed.), *Mass Communication, Democracy and Civil Society in Africa*, UNESCO-NATCOM, Lagos 1999, pp. 533–542; see also: 'Broadcasting in Nigeria: Unlocking the airwaves', in: *Media Rights Agenda and Article 19*, Lagos, 2001, p. 11.

Broadcasting licensees have to comply with broad obligations set by the National Mass Communication Policy of 1990. Among others they are bound to:

- Disseminate information to enhance people's welfare, provide professional and comprehensive coverage of Nigerian culture, opportunity for discussion of national issues, regulate channels of communication between the government and the people, effective coverage of the country, delivery of accurate information;
- Promote values of national consciousness, emphasise excellence in ethical and programme standards to meet the tastes of the viewing and listening public, including programming in indigenous languages to ensure direct relevance to local communities;
- Ensure that programmes for children and youth are used for inculcating in them indigenous values, spirit of hard work and patriotism.

The NBC complements these obligations with a framework of rules and procedures which it says are for 'developing and enhancing professionalism in Nigerian broadcasting'. It demands, for example, that broadcasters observe basic professional tenets such as caution, empathy and due sensitivity in the coverage of emergencies, calamities, riots, grief, etc. The failure to define, in consultation with industry stakeholders, such terms as 'caution', 'empathy' and 'sensitivity' has provided the NBC latitude to take arbitrary decisions against broadcasters. In one instance in 2005, the NBC closed down Africa Independent Television (AIT) over its coverage of a plane crash in Lisa-Igbore, a village in south-west Nigeria. The station was re-opened after public protests against the closure.

The NBC also obliges broadcasters to adhere to a number of laws such as the Official Secrets Act and provisions on sedition despite the fact that the latter have been pronounced unconstitutional by the Court of Appeal in 1983.

Failure to comply with licence conditions may attract any of seven categories of sanctions:

(a) reprimand
(b) warning
(c) right of reply
(d) light, heavy, severe and special case fine. Light fines range from N 50 000 to N 99 000, heavy fines from N 100 000 to N 999 999, severe fines upwards of N 1 000 000, while a special case fine attracts the breach value plus percentage penalty. The NBC unilaterally decides the monetary value of a breach along with the percentage penalty.

(e) reduction of broadcast hours

(f) suspension of licence

(g) revocation of licence.[62]

Broadcasters have been sanctioned on many occasions. Examples are: a warning to Murhi International TV (Lagos) in October 2005 over alleged breaches which include 'alarming reportage of dark clouds and fumes over Lagos which was used as 'breaking news' without verification or onsite report and unverifiable claims of traditional medicine'; a fine of N 500 000 on each of eleven state and commercial stations who violated guidelines on political coverage during the 2007 national elections; or the suspension of licences in early 2006 of six commercial stations who defaulted on the payment of licence renewal fees.

A licence may be revoked by the NBC if, for example, a licensee fails to pay prescribed fees on the due date or if the station has been used in a 'manner contrary to national interest'. This, experts say, could be used arbitrarily because government's and the public's definitions of 'national interest' often differ.[63] The regulatory body has used the national interest argument as a reason to close down a commercial radio station in 2003 in Benin City, in the south-south region. The NBC claimed that the station had aired martial music and that this could have been interpreted by the audience/public as an indication that there had been a military coup (martial music was the kind usually played by soldiers during coup d'etats in Nigeria). The station pointed out that it had been playing solemn classical Christian music as a mark of respect for a senior editor at the station who died in a car accident. The station was later re-opened.

The commission monitors broadcasting stations through a network of zonal and state offices as well as independent professionals located in various regions of the country. Reports are sent to the headquarters in Abuja, the country's capital. Sometimes, these reports are published in the regulator's journal, *NBC News*. In addition to monitoring aired programmes, zonal and state officers of the NBC make visits to stations to inspect facilities. Independent professionals used in monitoring are industry veterans, mainly those who have retired from active broadcasting. The regulatory body believes that their long professional experience is useful for the monitoring process.

---

62   See *Nigeria Broadcasting Code*, (4th Edition), 2006, pp. 101–104.
63   *Media Rights Agenda and Article 19*, op.cit., p. 14.

3   Complaints and conflict resolution systems

Complaints and conflict management mechanisms have been provided for in legislative and regulatory codes.

The Broadcasting Code is the industry regulation document. It was first published in 1993 by the NBC and is reviewed every three years, the last time in 2006.[64] An NBC code review committee takes inputs from industry stakeholders, produces a draft, sends it to stakeholders and discusses it with them during a retreat with the objective to adopt a revised document.

A station is expected to adhere to the commission's six-stage complaints and resolution procedure:

(a) An aggrieved person, group or institution lodges a complaint with the commission within 14 days after the occurrence of an act or omission.

(b) Upon receipt of complaint, the commission informs and requires the station to provide a response within 72 hours, although an extension of time may be given.

(c) Within 14 days after receipt of response from the station, the commission investigates and arbitrates.

(d) Then it notifies the parties to the complaint on the progress of its investigation, finding and reasons.

(e) If the complaint is upheld, the station is directed to comply with the findings (meaning: decisions) of the NBC 'within a specified time'.

(f) The findings are made public.

The process is handled entirely within the NBC. There is no separate or specially constituted complaints mechanism or a provision for appeals either within to the NBC or outside to the courts.

According to the code, a licensee is required to 'regularly broadcast information on how the public may lodge complaints about its programming'. The meaning of 'regularly' is not specified and stations simply ignore this requirement.

The NBC has expressed concern that members of the public seldom use the existing complaints mechanism, but records of the few cases where this has happened are not available to the public. Political parties, their candidates and state governments have been forwarding complaints, which have been investigated and arbitrated by the NBC.

---

64   At the time of writing the next review was under way.

4   Proposed merger of regulatory authorities

Under its establishment law, the NBC has the mandate to regulate only broadcasting. Telecommunication is regulated by the Nigerian Communications Commission (NCC) while information technology falls under the National Information Technology Development Agency (NITDA). The NCC and NITDA each have their own legislative framework.

In August 2006, government set up a presidential task force on the restructuring of government institutions/organisations in the telecommunications and ICT sector. This included the broadcasting sector. The task force is, among others, mandated to study the implications of having different supervisory agencies for content and infrastructure in the communications sector and to identify stages of convergence and the role of the legislator in the emerging convergence environment.

The task force has been working behind closed doors and results are not known yet. But what looked like one of the outcomes of the process in early 2007 was the merger of the hitherto ministry of information and national orientation with that of communications to form a new ministry of information and communication. Another government announcement in early 2008 said that the NBC and the NCC would be merged while two new ministries (one for information, the other for ICT) would be created from the current ministry of information and communication. Details of the proposed arrangement are still to be released although there is speculation that the new information ministry will just handle government's public information management machinery while the ICT ministry will be in charge of policy and implementation for the ICT sector and will supervise the regulatory body to be formed after the merger of the NBC and NCC.

While the public is waiting, this convergence issue has been a subject of discussion among stakeholders. Interest groups such as the Nigerian Computer Society, the Association of Licenced Telecommunication Operators of Nigeria (ALTON) and the Nigeria Internet Group (NIG) all support the merger of the regulatory bodies.

Broadcasters have also been positive toward the merger but warn that the interests of the broadcasting sector must be safeguarded. John Momoh, CEO of Channels TV, says that 'the government must ensure that the NBC is not made subordinate to the NCC in any merger arrangement'.[65] A former chairman of the NBC, Peter Enahoro, advocated a merger process characterised by a 'partnership of the merging regulatory bodies within one stable and not one swallowing or dissolving into the other'.[66]

The Nigerian Community Radio Coalition added that the proposed regulatory

---

65   J. Momoh, 'Secrets of Channels TV success', *Daily Independent*, 12 April 2007, p. E2.
66   'Proposed NBC/NCC merger: Union of uneven brands?', *ThisDay*, 12 March 2007 p. 64.

body should be independent and its administrative structure should be designed in a way that will allow for equitable attention to be given to all the sub-sectors, including broadcasting.[67]

5   Conclusions and recommendations

The regulatory structure and culture in place at the NBC is a vestige of military rule. The provisions of the law (NBC Act 38 and its amendment plus section 39(2) of the country's Constitution) and the broadcasting code constrain it from appropriately serving the public interest, helping to consolidate democracy and participating as an up-to-date regulator in the contemporary global broadcasting landscape.

The members of the NBC are all appointed by the president on the recommendation of the information minister. This procedure contradicts Clause 7 of the Declaration of Principles on Freedom of Expression in Africa, which requires that the appointment process for members of a regulatory body should be open and transparent and involve the participation of civil society, and shall not be controlled by any political party.

The NBC lacks independence and adequate protection against political and economic interference and is accountable to the executive arm of government.

The licensing procedures are shrouded in secrecy and the granting of licences is left to the discretion of the president.

Complaints and sanctions procedures concentrate all powers in the NBC, leaving no room for appeals and judicial processes.

Recommendations

- An updated broadcasting policy should be put in place. This should include the completion of the review process of the 1990 National Mass Communication Policy and updating of the broadcasting policy contained in that document, also taking into account the 2004 National Mass Communication Policy review draft and the 2006 Community Radio Policy Document.
- Section 39(2) of the country's Constitution, which gives the president power to authorise broadcasting licences, should be amended, such that this power will vest in the regulatory body.

---

67 *Roadmap to building a sustainable community radio sector in Nigeria: The Stakeholders' Charter*, Initiative on Building Community Radio in Nigeria, Lagos, 2005, p. 33.

- The NBC Act should be reviewed and deliver the following:
    - A converged regulatory body which should be independent and have an administrative structure designed in a way that will allow for equitable attention to all the subsectors, including broadcasting.
    - The regulatory body should be independent of the government, political parties and media interests.
    - Its members should be appointed by parliament in a transparent and public process which involves consultation with civil society and other specific constituencies from which the members are drawn. Government agencies, political parties and persons with financial interests in the industry should be disqualified from membership. Members of the NBC should be granted security of tenure.
    - The NBC should be vested with full regulatory powers, including the power to process applications and grant licences, without reference to government organs like the ministry of information and the presidency.
    - The commission should be accountable to the public through parliament.
    - It should be funded through direct budgetary allocation from parliament as well as from a share of radio/TV-set licence fees.
    - The licensing process should be transparent. Clear criteria and procedure for licensing, agreed upon in consultation with stakeholders, should be advertised by the NBC. Time limits should be set for the process, explanations should be supplied to unsuccessful applicants, and there should be provision for appeals through institutions such as the courts.
    - Political parties and owners of other media, particularly newspapers, should be ineligible for obtaining a broadcasting licence.
    - Religious organisations should be eligible for broadcasting licences subject to criteria such as: restriction of coverage to geographical and homogenous communities; a commitment to devote a substantial proportion of their airtime to secular public interest programming; and an undertaking that their content will not offend religious, ethnic and other sensibilities.

    –   Precise proportional stipulations of local and foreign content of broadcasters' programming should be removed from legislation and left for the consideration of the NBC in consultation with stakeholders.

    –   The complaints and sanctions process should be reviewed to guarantee:

        »   an appeals mechanism – through the establishment of either a broadcasting complaints body or a special, higher-level body within the regulator, as well as the courts;

        »   an industry consultative mechanism to undertake a periodic review of the proportionality of stations' offences to imposed sanctions.

- All the above reviews should be done with the participation of stakeholders and civil society at large.
- The on-going process of licensing private commercial broadcasting networks should be concluded and the federal government should, through the NBC, announce the results of the 2009 bid process.

6

Overview of the State Broadcasters

1   Legislation

State broadcasting is separated in law and administration into radio and television. The radio service is provided by the Federal Radio Corporation of Nigeria (FRCN) and the television service by the Nigerian Television Authority (NTA).

1.1   Radio

The FRCN was formally established through military law by the FRCN Decree 8 of 1979, even though it began operations a year earlier on 1 April 1978. Two subsidiary pieces of legislation, the FRCN (Amendment) Decree 9 and the FRCN (Amendment) Decree 14 were promulgated in 1988 and 1991 respectively. Under Nigeria's current democratic system, these decrees are now regarded and referred to as acts of parliament.

Section 5(1) of the FRCN Act mandates the corporation 'to provide as a public service in the interest of Nigeria, independent and impartial radio broadcasting services for general reception within Nigeria and to provide External Services for general reception in countries outside Nigeria'.

This is complemented by section 5(2) which stipulates that the corporation shall ensure that its services 'reflect the unity of Nigeria as a federation and at the same time give adequate expression to the culture, characteristics and affairs and opinions of each state or other part of the federation'.

Section 7 lists the corporation's functions as, amongst others, 'planning, regulating and coordinating the activities of the entire federal radio broadcasting system', 'maintaining high broadcasting standards in accordance with national policy', 'organizing, providing and subsidizing for the purpose of broadcasting educational activities and public entertainment', 'collecting news and information' and providing 'training, education and research services'. A 'national policy' as referred to in the act was articulated only 11 years later, in 1990, when the National Mass Communication Policy was released.

The FRCN reports to the information minister and is one of the government parastatals under the ministry of information and communication.

The membership of the corporation's 11-member board of directors is provided for in section 2(1) of the act. the board comprises a chairman, the director-general of the Corporation, a representative each of the ministry of information and the ministry of external affairs, a representative of women's interests, and six other persons with requisite experience in mass media, education, management, financial matters, engineering, and arts and culture.

All members, including the director-general of the corporation, are appointed by the information minister with prior approval by the Federal Executive Council.

Each member who is not a public officer holds office for three years and the term of office can be renewed for a further three years. Members who are public officers have indefinite tenure.

Section 3 of the Act lists a number of reasons why the information minister may remove a member before expiry of his/her tenure: misconduct and inability to perform the functions of office; absence from two consecutive meetings (and if the explanation given is not accepted by the corporation); or expression by the corporation that the member's continued presence is not in the national interest or the interest of the corporation.

In May 2009, government announced a ten-member governing body for the corporation without giving details of the background of or constituencies represented by the appointees except for the one slot retained for a representative of the federal ministry of information and communication (for which no particular individual name was given). Two of the members have a media background: a senior journalist who worked in the presidency in the early part of the present administration (2007–2008) and a former media aide to the immediate past president of the country.

In addition to the appointment and removal of members of the governing body, the Act gives the information minister and other government office holders further powers.

In terms of section 14 the information minister can issue directives to the Corporation. This power was strengthened by FRCN (Amendment) Act 14 of 1991. It provides that the minister may give the FRCN directives not only of a general character but also relating to particular matters regarding the performance of the functions of the Corporation. The Corporation must comply with such directives.

Section 9(a) and (b) provide that the corporation shall broadcast, 'as may appear to the corporation to be desirable in the public interest, speeches of the Supreme Military Council, National Council of States and Federal Executive Council' as well as 'matters of any kind (including religious services or ceremonies) relating to or representing the main streams of religious thought or belief in Nigeria'.

According to section 10, the corporation shall, whenever so requested by an 'authorized public officer', broadcast a government programme, at the corporation's own expense.

The appointment of members to the governing board of a supposedly public institution by government without any provision for public consultation, let alone participation, renders the process arbitrary and lacking in transparency. The presence of government representatives on the board and the involvement of the information minister, the Federal Executive Council or 'authorized public officers' in virtually all issues of the corporation's governance and programming leaves no insulation against political or economic interference, sweeps away editorial independence and shuts the door against accountability through the legislature. In the final analysis, all these provisions turn the FRCN into a government mouthpiece.

1.2 Television

The Nigerian Television Authority (NTA) was established through another military law, the Nigerian Television Authority Decree (now Act) 24 of 1977, a year after the Authority had begun operations.

The Act describes functions similar to those outlined for the radio broadcaster in the FRCN Act. Sections 6(1) and (2) mandate the authority to 'provide as a public service in the interest of Nigeria, independent and impartial television broadcasting for general reception in Nigeria' and to ensure that its services 'reflect the unity of Nigeria as a Federation and at the same time give adequate expression to the culture, characteristics and affairs of each state, zone or other part of the federation'.

Section 9 requires the authority to ensure that its programming maintains, among other things, proper balance and high quality, preserves impartiality in respect of matters of political or industrial controversy, and excludes materials likely to offend against good taste and decency or designed to serve the interests of a political party. Because 'good taste and decency' are not defined, the interpretation remains open to arbitrary decisions of government.

The governing board of the authority consists of a chairman and 14 other members: the six chairmen of the zonal boards (see below), the director-general, one representative of women's organisations, and six other experienced persons drawn from the mass media, education, management, financial matters, engineering, and arts and culture fields. The National Council of Ministers (Federal Executive Council) is empowered by section 2(2) to reduce, increase or otherwise vary the composition of this membership.

All members – including the director-general of the broadcaster – are appointed by the National Council of Ministers on the recommendation of the information minister. The tenure of government representatives is indefinite while other members serve for a term of three years, with the possibility of re-appointment for a further three years. The length of tenure of the director-general is not specified. As in the case of the radio broadcaster's board and for the same grounds as outlined in the FRCN Act quoted above, the information minister is entitled to remove board members, again including the director-general, at any time before completion of their terms.

The functions of the governing board are not spelt out in the law. The last board was dissolved after a new government took office in 2007 and a replacement was constituted only in May 2009. The new board has 17 members, including the Corporation's director-general and seven executive directors. One seat on the board has been given to the federal ministry of information and communication – without attachment of any individual name or particular designation. Among the other eight members, whose constituencies or the interests they represent were not specified, are two with a media background: a former chairman of the authority and a former staff member of the *Guardian* newspaper in Lagos.

The information minister is empowered by section 13 to give directives either of a general character or relating to particular matters, and the Authority must comply with such directives. As is the case with the FRCN, it is mandatory for the television broadcaster to provide coverage for the speeches of key government officials such as ministers and legislators, as well as events such as services or ceremonies of the main streams of religious thought or belief in Nigeria. Under section 12, a 'special programme' shall be broadcast if so directed by the information minister. The law does not specify what such a 'special programme' might be and thus leaves the definition to the minister's discretion.

The act creates a second layer of governance through the so-called zonal boards. Section 14 says that for the purposes of 'variety' and better reception of its programmes the Authority shall divide the country into six zones, each of which shall have its own zonal board.

Each zonal board shall consist of six to eight members, including the chairman, appointed by the information minister after consultation with the governors of the represented states and with the approval of the National Council of Ministers. A member of the zonal board shall be a person appearing to the minister to have wide knowledge and experience in such fields as newspapers, broadcasting and other media or mass communication; cultural, economic and religious affairs of the zones; the creative arts, education and financial matters; as well as business and industry. Members are appointed for three years and eligible for re-appointment.

This division into zones with their respective boards is no longer in place. Instead, network centres have been introduced in recent years, which do not represent the zones specified in the law.

As in the case of the FRCN, the framework of control of the NTA concentrates key powers in the hands of government ministers, gives room for arbitrariness, is characterised by a lack of transparency, and has the overall effect of depriving the organisation of any independence and turning it into the voice of government and its officials.

2   Profile of the state broadcasters

State/public broadcasters exist at two levels: those owned by the federal government and by the state (second tier) governments respectively. At the federal level are the Federal Radio Corporation of Nigeria (FRCN) and the Nigerian Television Authority (NTA). There is also the Voice of Nigeria (VON), the country's international radio broadcaster.

2.1   Radio

The FRCN operates a network of 41 FM stations (29 functioning, 12 yet to go on air), each with its own programming, along with four short wave national stations located in Gwagwalada-Abuja (federal capital territory), Enugu in the south-east, Kaduna in the north-west and Ibadan in the south-west. SW stations are also being planned for yet-to-be announced locations in the north-east and south-south (the Niger Delta). The state governments own and run a total of 39 radio stations.

FRCN claims to be 'reaching an estimated 120 million listeners, broadcasting in English and 15 local languages'.[68]

The corporation classifies its programmes into news and non-news. News programmes consist of news and current affairs. Non-news programmes comprise culture, public entertainment (e.g. drama, music, comedy), 'public enlightenment' (e.g. documentary, discussion, magazine, feature) and family support, among others.[69]

---

68   See *FRCN Today*, a publication of the Federal Radio Corporation of Nigeria (undated), p. 3.
69   Ibid., p. 7.

2.2 Television

The Nigerian Television Authority (NTA) runs one national channel and has a national network of 101 stations, of which 89 are on air while others are at various stages of completion. They are located in the various states and Abuja, the federal capital, and have their own programming but also links to network programming. Eight of these stations are designated zonal network centres. A zonal network centre is a station which coordinates operations of a number of other stations and through which network programmes for its zone are linked to the national network programming of the Authority.

The second tier of government (the states) along with the administration of the federal capital territory control 37 stations.

Officials of the Authority claim that its services are reaching between 60 and 90 million viewers but this is not supported by any independent audience research.

3   Organisational structures

3.1   Radio

At the top of the governance structure of the FRCN is the board of directors. The director-general is assisted by two governance structures: the first comprises zonal directors in the four national stations (who also supervise the FRCN FM stations in their respective zones) and the director of Lagos operations. The second consists of directors and heads at headquarters in Abuja responsible for the following directorates or departments: programmes, news, administration/supplies, finance/accounts, marketing, training, engineering, special duties, legal adviser/secretary, internal audit, and corporate development and communication.

Responsibility for the day-to-day running of the corporation is in the hands of a central management committee (CMC) which comprises the director-general, all other directors and the company secretary.

There are also committees of management (COMs) at headquarters and national stations' levels. At headquarters, the COM comprises directors and heads of departments, with the most senior chairing. In the case of national stations and Lagos operations, these committees consist of heads of sub-directorates, general managers of FM stations and the internal audit department, headed by the respective executive director.

Decisions on potentially controversial issues or material are taken by the top management. From the level of editors they are referred upward to supervisors, i.e.

the manager (news), and from there to the deputy director (news). If he/she is still unable to resolve the issue, it will be referred to the director (news), who takes the final decision. However, professional decision-making is limited by interference from the information ministry which frequently issues circulars with directives to the corporation's management.

These include press releases and announcements/adverts which the ministry wants aired on the radio network. Management does not seem to regard this as a form of pressure or limitation of their editorial freedom.[70] Also, in the absence of a board, the director-general referred issues beyond his approval level (e.g. promotion of senior personnel) to the minister.

Editorial decisions are also determined by commercial considerations. For example, the FRCN actually sells news space: for a fee, individuals or organisations can get their events covered and presented as part of the news bulletins without any indication that these stories are paid news. This opportunity is frequently used by companies and other businesses as well as government agencies. The FRCN thus cedes editorial control and vital public space to the highest bidder.

The corporation has a staff of about 2 600 (exact figures not available), with 283 working in the news directorate and 430 in programmes. Together these two directorates account for up to 60 per cent of senior staff, those at levels from grade level (GL) 08, the entry point for bachelor degree holders fresh from university.

Remuneration is in line with the government civil service salary structure, following a strict hierarchy from assistant officers at the bottom via several ranks of officer up to principal, on to managers and at the top several layers of directorial positions. Salary levels begin with a GL 01 and go up to GL 17. Within this structure, for example, an officer Grade 11 (e.g. a reporter, producer or editor) is on GL 08 and gets a total annual package (salary plus allowances) of N 441 875 (US$ 3 776 – as at April 2008), his senior on GL 12 (principal reporters, producers, editors) collects N 709 224 (US$ 6 061) while anyone at the top level of GL 17 (director) takes home N 1 807 992 (US$ 15 452).

These salary packages are fairly low in the Nigerian context. In comparison, commercial broadcasting stations keep their remuneration scales secret, but confidential information indicates that they vary considerably from one company to another. A fresh entrant's (bachelor degree holder) annual pay ranges from about N 350 000 (US$ 2 991) to N 660 000 (US$ 5 641) per annum. At organisations like Raypower FM and Africa Independent Television, an entry-level reporter earns about N 660 000 (US$ 5 641) and a manager (news) as much as N 3 600 000 (US$ 30 769) per annum.

---

70 Ibid.

Journalists who want to join the FRCN need a bachelor's degree from a university, not necessarily in journalism or mass communication. Specialised training is available for beginners at the corporation's training school in Lagos. There have been complaints from staff that this school is hampered by lack of vital modern training equipment particularly in new information and communication technologies (ICTs).

3.2 Television

The organisational structure of the NTA follows a three tier hierarchy from the national (headquarters) level via the level of zonal network centres down to the level of individual stations.

At the top of the national/headquarters structure is the governing board, to which the director-general reports – or rather: is supposed to report, given that no such board existed at the time of writing. The director-general is assisted by seven executive directors heading the directorates of programmes, news, marketing, finance and administration, special projects, training and capacity building, and engineering as well as a secretary/legal adviser.

Zonal general managers (ZGMs) head zonal/network centres and report directly to the director-general at headquarters. At the helm of affairs in the stations are general managers (GMs) who, in turn, report to the zonal general managers.

Controversial editorial decisions are handled by high echelons in the news directorate. An editorial board conference chaired by the executive director (news) and comprising senior editorial staff decides on events and issues to be covered. Should there be any issue with potential for controversy, the executive director (news) passes it to the director-general.

As is the case with radio, the NTA also sells news space for a fee without indicating that such stories have been paid for.

The Authority has had a staff strength of less than 4 000 (exact figures are not available) for more than 12 years, during which time it expanded from 27 to 101 stations and began 24-hour transmission in most of them.

The news and programmes directorates currently have the largest numbers of staff, while administration has undergone substantial retrenchments when management adopted an outsourcing policy for jobs in such areas as cleaning and security, among others.

Due to a freeze on recruitment, staff are overstretched and overworked. Jobs meant for three or four persons are now being done by one. Shift duties have been collapsed from three into two segments, which means that an eight-hour shift now runs for 12 hours without additional remuneration. In many stations, managements resort to casualisation, a system of engaging a professional on a day-by-day basis which entitles him/her to only the daily fee and no other welfare benefits or employer commitments. People are not being promoted to higher grades, although an employee in the civil service is eligible for promotion every three years. As it is, however, many are occupying the same position for much longer periods and keep hoping that management will address the situation soon. Salary structures are similar to those at the FRCN.

Journalists who want to join the NTA need a national diploma, a certificate acquired after two years of post-secondary school education. In addition to pre-entry training, further capacity-building facilities are provided for the Authority's journalists/broadcasters at its television college, which also awards degrees. Staffers in other fields such as administration, marketing or finance are sponsored for training programmes organised by professional institutions like the Administrative Staff College of Nigeria (ASCON) and the Nigerian Institute of Management (NIM). Members of the staff interviewed say the training acquired at the TV college and the other training institutions is relevant to their jobs.

4   Attitudes within the state broadcasters towards public broadcasting

4.1   Radio

During interviews at the FRCN, the attitudes of staff members towards the concept of public broadcasting varied between defining it as 'state-owned and state-funded broadcasting' and 'a medium through which the governed are informed and educated on the policies and activities of government'.

The generality of citizens (whose taxes are being used to fund the organisation) is thought to be the prime institution which should hold a public broadcaster accountable. Specific public bodies such as an ombudsman or regulators like the National Broadcasting Commission are also considered capable to perform this role.

Government is assigned a supervisory and supporting role in relation to the public broadcaster. It should not interfere in the administrative and editorial management but provide adequate funding for operations and enact appropriate legislation which would enhance the professional running of the organisation.

Some think that the role of a public broadcaster in relation to the government is properly served through informing the public on government's activities, sensitising them towards government policies and programmes and generating feedback. Others say that the public broadcaster should set the agenda for government and hold it accountable to the people through objective and balanced programming.

There was agreement that all political parties should get fair and dispassionate coverage. The ruling party should never be favoured above others. Parties should also be held accountable on their election manifestos when they get into power.

Civil society is considered a key stakeholder in public broadcasting. Its voices should be heard and positions adequately reflected in the programming of the public broadcaster.

Some believe that a public broadcaster should reflect the full spectrum of public opinions and concerns on issues. Others argue that on issues involving the security of the country the broadcaster must be selective.

Diverse interpretations are given to the concept of 'public interest'. Some say the public interest is served when government is criticised or commended at appropriate times. Others say that for the public interest to be served, editorial decisions must be favourable to the majority of the people, while conceding that 'majority' may be a relative and subjective thing.

4.2 Television

Professionals in the NTA convey their understanding of the concept of public broadcasting in similar ways: in summary, they see it as the dissemination of information on activities of government agencies and functionaries which impact on the lives of the people. They add that in Nigeria the dissemination process is itself controlled by the state.

There is agreement that some office or institution should hold a public broadcaster accountable, but while some say this should be parliament others insist it should be a kind of public trustee, a body which represents the interests of the people of the country.

Many ascribe the role of 'facilitator' or 'regulator' to the government in relation to the public broadcaster. In these roles, they expect government to allocate adequate funds and provide basic infrastructure to the broadcaster, create an environment of easy access to government-held information to its journalists and remove 'gagging' completely.

A school of thought within the broadcaster believes the NTA should be a watchdog, that is, act as a check on the activities or possible excesses of government. Another school says the broadcaster should concentrate on explaining government's programmes and activities to the people. This latter school agrees that it would be professionally correct, for example, for the public broadcaster to allow the president regular airtime to explain the work of government to the public. The first school says this would be an abuse or unfair use of the media, and that the appropriate response to such a request should be a refusal.

All professionals interviewed want the broadcaster to give equal and fair coverage to the activities of political parties. It should also provide a check on them.

Civil society should act as whistleblowers, supplying information on corrupt practices for dissemination by the broadcaster, and as a constant check against government's misuse of the broadcaster.

There is consensus that the public broadcaster should reflect the full spectrum of public opinion on issues. Events or issues are taken to be of 'public interest' when they directly affect the generality of the citizens. Issues such as health, education, water supply, agriculture, and security are cited as examples.

5   Conclusions and recommendations

The Declaration of Principles on Freedom of Expression in Africa says in its article VI:

> State and government controlled broadcasters should be transformed into public service broadcasters, accountable to the public through the legislature rather than the government, in accordance with the following principles:
> - public broadcasters should be governed by a board which is protected against interference, particularly of a political or economic nature;
> - the editorial independence of public service broadcasters should be guaranteed
> ...

Going by this definition, neither the FRCN nor the NTA can be described as public broadcasters. From their founding legislation, through the administrative structures and running of the organisations, to the service conditions and general welfare of their personnel, they are clearly positioned as state broadcasters.

A governing body appointed at the pleasure of government officials through processes that lack transparency can only be loyal to the government, not the people. An organisation subject to government interference already prescribed in law can only be the voice of government. A structure immersed in the constricting civil service culture cannot compete in the professional broadcasting world of the 21st century.

Recommendations

The NBC plays an important role in Nigerians' lives. The following recommendations will assist in ensuring that the public broadcaster meets the public's expectations:

- Existing legislation for the two state broadcasters – the NTA Act 24 of 1977 and FRCN Act of 1979 (with its amendments) – should be replaced by a new act establishing Radio and Television Nigeria as genuine public service broadcasters.
- The new legislation should be developed through a broad consultation process with the participation of all interested stakeholders and the public at large.
- The new legislation should establish the public broadcaster as an independent legal entity with editorial independence and strong safeguards against any interference from the federal government, state governments and other interests.
- The public broadcaster should be governed by a board established and acting according to the following principles:
    - appointment procedures should be open, transparent and free from political interference;
    - the board should represent a broad cross-section of the nigerian population;
    - its role should be clearly set out in law and its main responsibility should be to ensure that the public broadcaster fulfils its mandate in the public interest and is protected against undue political or commercial influences;
    - the board should not interfere in the day-to-day decision-making of the broadcaster, especially in relation to broadcast content, and respect the principle of editorial independence.
- Even prior to the enactment of new legislation and the setting up of a new board the following priorities should be given urgent attention:
    - commercial and editorial decisions should be separated to prevent conflict of interest, and the practice of accepting 'news' paid for by institutions, business, government or others should be stopped;
    - the directorate of news should be enabled to take autonomous decisions. its director should be the editor-in-chief, whose judgments will be based on criteria of newsworthiness and not on commercial considerations;
    - an audit of organisational structures should be undertaken with the aim of discarding inappropriate and inflexible civil service hierarchies and conditions of service (including salaries) and turning the corporation(s) into modern broadcasters able to compete in a fast-changing media environment.

7

Funding of the State Broadcasters

1 Main sources of funding

Paragraph 1(b) of the fourth schedule to the 1999 Nigerian Constitution provides for the collection of licence fees for ownership of radio and television sets. It makes the local governments (the third tier of government, 774 in all) the collecting authorities but does not stipulate who the beneficiaries of these fees are to be.

Section 7 of the National Broadcasting Commission (NBC) (Amendment) Act 55 of 1999, on the other hand, empowers the regulatory body to 'collect and hold in trust for or disburse on behalf of the broadcast houses such licence fees accruing from ownership of radio and television sets, as the commission may prescribe'.

Obviously, the Constitution is the supreme law and the general legal principle applies that any provision in any specific law which is inconsistent with the Constitution shall be null and void to the extent of its inconsistency. On this basis many local government councils in several states have been collecting the fees from owners of television and radio sets and spending them as part of their normal revenues, without disbursing any portion to the NBC or the individual radio and television stations.

1.1 Television

Details of the National Television Authority's (NTA) income and finances are generally not available and treated as closely guarded secrets. Nevertheless, it is common knowledge that the Authority draws grants (called subventions) from government every year as part of its funding. These are one of the three main sources of funding for the NTA prescribed by sections 23 and 24 of the NTA Act. The others are 'such sums as may from time to time be lent to the Authority by any persons' (i.e. loans), and 'such sums as may be collected or received by the Authority from other sources either in the execution of its functions or in respect of any property vested in the Authority or otherwise howsoever', for example income from advertisements, property investments, etc.

The allocation of the government grant goes through a long process of assessment. The Authority prepares and sends its funding requirements to the information ministry, where these are further assessed, incorporated into the ministry's overall funding package, and forwarded to the presidency's budgeting department. After further assessment, the grant becomes part of the President's Appropriation Bill submitted to parliament for approval and sent back to the president for assent. Whatever the amount approved is then channelled from the presidency through the same route to the authority and accessed monthly.

NTA officials complain that the grants have dwindled in recent years, while shortfalls of between 15 and 25 per cent in the monthly releases have also been very common. As a result, payment of staff salaries and acquisition of equipment for programming are often difficult.

The broadcaster sometimes receives government support through other channels or arrangements. When it moved its headquarters from Lagos to Abuja, the new federal capital, the new buildings were constructed by the administration of the federal capital territory. When the country hosted the All-Africa Games in 2003, the government provided special funds for equipment to enable the Authority to give adequate coverage to the tournament.

Advertisements and sponsorships constitute another major funding source. Given plummeting government grants, income thus generated now appears to be the broadcaster's prime revenue.

The NTA has a variety of rates on its commercial sheets. For example, a 60-second advert between 20h00 and 20h30 is charged at N 150 000 (US$ 1 282), while a same-length slot during the 21h00 news costs N 500 000 (US$ 4 273). The broadcaster airs at least nine adverts during the one-hour programme. For sponsorships, airtime charges are N 750 000 (US$ 6 410) for 30 minutes and N 1 300 000 (US$ 11 111) for 60 minutes with an additional handling charge of 50 per cent.

Although figures are not available on the proportion of total ad-spend which goes to the NTA, it can be assumed that the broadcaster's size and country-wide coverage give it a decisive advantage over other players in the market. It is therefore not surprising that competitors, particularly the commercial broadcasters grouped under the umbrella of the Independent Broadcasters Association of Nigeria (IBAN), have called for the NTA to make do with government subsidies and stay out of the advertising market altogether.

Instead, the Authority has become increasingly aggressive in its efforts to generate funds from advertising and other commercial activities, and the adverse effects on editorial independence and programming are clearly visible.

Under the heading 'News of Special Interest', the NTA broadcasts commercialised, paid-for news during at least four major news bulletins without alerting viewers by clearly indicating them as such. The charge for airing such items is N 200 000 (US$ 1 709) during the 16h00 and 19h00 news bulletins, N 500 000 (US$ 4 273) during the 21h00 news (Monday to Saturday) and N 650 000 (US$ 5 555) during the 21h00 *Newsline* on Sunday.

The broadcaster also charges interviewees for appearing on its shows. Participation in major interview programmes such as *One-on-One* (one hour twice a week) costs N 750 000 (US$ 6 410), while in others, like *Periscope*, it can be had at a cheaper price of N 200 000 (US$ 1 709).

Another source of income is the sale of airtime for live coverage of events. Individuals or businesses who would like to have any activity organised by them broadcast live on national television will pay N 3 million (US$ 25 641), N 5 million (US$ 42 735) and N 6 million (US$ 51 282) for one, two and three hours respectively.

In addition to these various ways of selling airtime to whoever can afford to buy it, the broadcaster is also seeking to generate additional funds in a number of other ways. In early 2008 it launched a subsidiary, TV Enterprises, whose mandate is to 'explore untapped potentials of the broadcast industry, media brokerage, actualization of the purchase of broadcast rights, concept initiation and collaborations'. TV Enterprises provide services in marketing (e.g. organisation of fairs or contests), production (e.g. of special documentaries) and publications (e.g. design and printing of books, diaries, promotional material).[71]

Another subsidiary, NTA Properties Investment Company Ltd, engages in the real-estate business.

The key challenge for the organisation in sourcing adequate funding is the absence of clear policy frameworks. The proposed commercialisation policy has been on the table for about 20 years without government ever finalising it. In its attempt to balance the books the NTA is working to a large extent in a legal vacuum, trying to generate as much income as it can by whatever means to make up for dwindling government support, while at the same time continuing to expand through the establishment of more stations.

With more time given to adverts and paid-for news taking up additional space, there is ever less room for the dissemination of unbiased information to the public. With more and more programme slots given over to paying customers to use as they please, the voices and agendas of business and other partisan social players with sufficient financial muscle are crowding out the voices of the public. Commercialisation in its

---

71   See *Television Enterprises: A Corporate Profile* (undated), a publication of TV Enterprises, p. 2.

present, aggressive form is clearly compromising the public mandate of the broadcaster
and has the potential of damaging its credibility beyond repair.

1.2 Radio

As stipulated in the FRCN Act, the FRCN also receives public funds (tax payers'
money), mainly in the form of grants. The process of determining and disbursing
these grants is similar to that outlined for the NTA above.

Figures on the amount of grants received or on the proportion of grants as part of
overall income are not available. The corporation has complained in recent years that
these grants are inadequate.

Some indirect support is given by government and other agencies. Radio House, the
FRCN's multi-storey headquarters in Abuja, the federal capital, which – incidentally
– also houses the information ministry, was built by the government. Recently the
Japanese government donated a transmitter.

Advertisements and sponsorships constitute a major source of funding for
the FRCN. Again, precise figures regarding total revenue from this source or its
proportion of overall income are not available. What is public knowledge, though,
is the fact that the radio broadcaster has an even more structured rate card than its
television counterpart.

A 60-second advert during the 07h00 news costs N 164 000 (US$ 1 401) and
N 25 000 (US$ 213) on the evening programmes. There are three categories of
commercial-in-news slots (i.e. commercials packaged as news): companies quoted on
the stock exchange and Grade 'A' parastatals (e.g. the Nigerian National Petroleum
Corporation) pay N 166 000 (US$ 1 418) per news story, state governments and other
agencies pay N 83 000 (US$ 709), and charity and non-profit organisations pay
N 58 000 (US$ 495). Costs of sponsored items vary depending on the time and the
type of programme they are slotted into (news bulletins or others) and range from
N 75 000 (US$ 641) to N350 000 (US$ 2 991). Participation in programmes such as
Radio Link, a Saturday morning interview programme, costs N 500 000 (US$ 4 273).
Live coverage of an event (per hour) can be bought for N 750 000 (US$ 6 410) in Abuja
and N 1 000 000 (US$ 8 547) outside Abuja.

There are no figures available on the split of total ad-spend between FRCN and
the other radio broadcasters. While commercial operators seem to be marketing
themselves more aggressively, the extensive network coverage of the FRCN still gives
it an advantage with advertisers who want to reach cross-regional or country-wide
audiences. On the other hand, the FRCN is still recovering from the loss of patronage
it experienced during the years of military rule in the country. This means it is not

the first choice of many advertisers, except those who particularly desire extensive geographical coverage which commercial stations cannot provide.

As in the case of television, other operators, particularly the commercial ones, have expressed opposition to the FRCN's competition for advertising. The argument remains that the state broadcaster should not be receiving government subsidies and earning income from the market at the same time, because this creates an uneven playing field.

Faced with inadequate funding from traditional sources, the FRCN has embarked on new areas of revenue generation. It has, for example, established Radio Nigeria Investments Ltd, a subsidiary expected to engage in various types of business, such as real-estate development, the promotion of up-and-coming and star artists, and the establishment and operation of cybercafés. The corporation is contemplating such other measures as encouraging its new FM stations located in remote areas to open city offices and studios to make them commercially viable, and national stations to explore the possibility of renting out their studios for commercial productions, as well as strengthening the synergies among news, marketing and programmes directorates to boost revenues.

Over the past five years, the management of the organisation has repeatedly complained of inadequate funding, particularly given its expansion programme, which involves the establishment of 32 new stations across the country. Although this is being done according to government instructions, the organisation is currently having to carry the financial burden without any additional support from the fiscus.

2   Spending

There are no figures available on the budgets and spending profiles of the NTA and the FRCN. Such information is regarded as secret.

3   Conclusions and recommendations

The Declaration of Principles on Freedom of Expression in Africa in its clause VI says that 'public broadcasters should be adequately funded in a manner that protects them from arbitrary interference with their budgets'.

The two main sources of income for the state broadcasters – government grants and advertisements/sponsorships – do not comply with this principle. Depending on these clearly impinges on the independence of the NTA and FRCN. Due to the unpredictability and inadequacy of grants from government, sufficient resources will not be available for activities at the appropriate times. In their desperation to shore up revenues through the market, the organisations end up ceding editorial control to business and other interests with the money to buy and influence programming.

Various ideas have been canvassed to improve the funding profiles of the two organisations. One of these, a modification of the existing system, is for government to provide 50 per cent of the public broadcasters' annual requirements through a statutory budgeting provision rather than a discretionary grant. The remaining 50 per cent is to be covered from commercial advertising, which should exclude all forms of sponsorship. In the event of a shortfall, the broadcasters should borrow from the money market. Another proposal, championed by the Independent Broadcasters Association of Nigeria (IBAN), says the public broadcasters should make do with government subsidies and leave the market to commercial operators.

Still another school suggests the selling or leasing out of some of the broadcasters' subsidiaries, as well as the splitting of the organisations into public and commercial channels under separate management structures. The public channels would be funded mainly through government grants and some subsidies from the commercial arms. The commercial channels would be commercially driven and funded by advertising.

Recommendations

- The entire system of funding for the NTA and FRCN needs to be thoroughly reviewed to guarantee their financial independence. To this end:
    - the corporations' financial status (sources of income and spending) should be examined by an independent accounting firm and be opened up to public scrutiny;
    - programme policies must be revisited and the broadcasters must assume full and exclusive editorial control over news and current affairs in particular;
    - on the basis of new programme policies and new organisational structures designed to implement them, business plans must be developed which reflect the financial needs of the NTA and FRCN and potential sources of revenue.
- The NTA and FRCN should derive their funding from a mix of broadcast licence fees, government grants and (to a limited extent) advertisements.
- Regarding licence fees it is recommended that:
    - the collecting agencies should be the government revenue

agencies. The overall licence fee revenue will go to the National Broadcasting Commission for distribution to broadcasters in the public, commercial and community subsectors;

- fee amounts should be is set in a way that allows for stable, predictable multi-year funding, enabling the broadcasters to plan and implement the necessary investment in programming and operational improvements.

- In regard to revenues from the state treasury it is recommended that:
  - an independent panel of experts determine the amount of subsidies needed by the NTA and FRCN over a three-year period to fulfill their public broadcasting mandate;
  - the National Assembly fund the public broadcasters directly (and not through a ministry or department) on the basis of the amount determined by the panel of experts, with the monies to be disbursed annually.

- Concerning advertisements and sponsorships it is recommended that:
  - The NTA and FRCN develop clear and strict guidelines on soliciting advertisements and conditions for accepting advertisements and programme sponsorships that will safeguard the broadcasters' editorial independence;
  - the broadcasting regulator embark on a process of public consultation with the objective to set appropriate limits to advertising and sponsorship on the NTA and FRCN.

8

Programming

1 Programme policies and guidelines

The Nigeria Broadcasting Code issued by the National Broadcasting Commission (NBC) is the prime programming document for all broadcasting organisations – be they state or private, radio or television. The code sets out a number of broad and more specific requirements that all broadcasters need to comply with.

On TV, foreign-language programmes should be transmitted with sub-titles in the official language (English) and national transmission of Nigerian-language programmes should also have sub-titles in English. Movies classified as not suitable for broadcast (NSFB) and music classified as not to be broadcast (NTBB) by the Nigerian Film and Video Censors Board should not be broadcast. Persons under the age of 18, especially vulnerable groups should be protected from offensive and harmful contents.

The code stipulates that all programmes adhere to the general principles of legality, decency and truthfulness. In particular, it calls for:

- accuracy, objectivity and fairness in the presentation of information;
- integrity: believable and credible programming, guarantee of a right of reply, compliance with laws including those relating to copyright, sedition and libel;
- authenticity: fiction should not be presented as real while archival, library or contrived materials should be clearly identified;
- good taste and decency: avoidance of obscene, indecent and vulgar language, and promotion of the sanctity of marriage and family life;
- the presentation of 'womanhood with respect and dignity'.

The code also addresses programming dealing with sensitive or potentially controversial subject matter, and lays down a number of specific requirements:

- Religious programming: among others, there must be equal opportunities and equitable airtime; not less than 90 minutes of a station's weekly airtime to be made available to all the religious groups in the community as a civil responsibility without charge; such programming should not contain an attack on or ridicule of another religion or sect; should present claims, especially those relating to miracles, in such a manner that is provable and believable. (The commission has now put a wholesale ban on broadcasting miracles.)
- Political broadcasting during elections: provision of 'equal time to all political parties'; ending broadcasting of election campaign materials not later than 24 hours before polling day; broadcasting election results only as announced by the authorised electoral officer.
- Coverage of crises and emergencies: morbid or graphic details of injuries, pain and agony should not be broadcast, 'except where it is useful in the resolution of attendant issues'; information provided must include particulars on evacuation, public safety, relief sites and shelters.

The Federal Radio Corporation of Nigeria (FRCN) is presently developing a set of programme/editorial policies and guidelines. Private stations complement the official code with in-house guidelines (mostly unwritten). For example, at Murhi International Television (MITV) these guidelines include a dress code (presenters should be well attired in indigenous dresses or western-type suits), punctuality (an anchor of a live programme must be at the station at least 30 minutes before start of programme), and the injunction for reporters not just to lift stories from newspapers or other media – they must verify the content.

2   Programming of state broadcasters

2.1 Nigerian Television Authority

The NTA provides central programming for all its stations (network service). All stations must broadcast the mandatory programmes but have a choice of broadcasting their own content in the periods from 06h00 to 06h30, 09h00 to 12h00, 13h00 to 13h30, 17h00 to 18h30, 19h00 to 20h00, midnight to 01h00 and 02h00 to 06h00.

Network programmes on the 24-hour schedule are generally in English and include the following:

- News:
    - *NTA News International*: 01h00–01h58, incorporating national and international news
    - *World News*: 04h00–04h25
    - *Nationwide*: 04h00–04h55, carrying local and international news
    - *NTA News*: 21h00–21h58, the flagship bulletin, containing local and international news. The Wednesday edition of this bulletin (called *NTA News Extra*) and the Sunday version (*Newsline*) run for one-and-a-half hours.
    - The local stations air their own local 25-minute news bulletins at 13h00 and 19h00.
- Current affairs (examples):
    - *Platform*: 11h00–11h55 on Tuesdays, an interview programme in which representatives of various agencies answer questions on the activities of their organisations. One recent edition, for example, featured the head of the military pensions board.
    - *Tuesday Live*: 23h00 on Tuesdays, a one-and-a-half hour discussion programme on contemporary issues of national interest.
    - *One-on-One*: 13h30 on Wednesdays and 11:00 on Fridays, a one-and-a-half hour interview programme with public officers.
    - *From the National Assembly*: 23h00–01h00 two days a week, a live transmission of proceedings in the chambers of the federal parliament – the Senate on Wednesdays, and House of Representative on Thursdays.
- Magazine type programmes: The most prominent is *AM Express* from 06h30 to 08h30, featuring a local news bulletin, headlines of major national newspapers, documentaries on places of cultural importance in various parts of the country, interviews, music, etc.
- Documentaries: At least one daily, such as:
    - *Documentary*: on state government activities, broadcast at 22h30 on Mondays for 25 minutes;
    - *Heritage*: a 20-minute slot at 22h00 on Thursdays, focusing on cultural issues across the country.

- Drama: There is at least one episode daily.
  - Countrywide NTA broadcasts *Stand Up Nigeria*, a 20-minute comedy at 09h00 on Tuesdays, and *Super Story*, a 50–minute soap at 20h05 on Thursdays.
  - Local station programmes complement these offerings with, among others, *New Papa Ajasco*, a 28-minute drama at 19h30 on Mondays and *So Wrong, So Wright*, a 25-minute programme at 19h30 on Wednesdays.
- Quiz/game shows:
  - *Flying High*, a 55-minute programme for young people at 14h00 on Tuesdays;
  - *Who Wants to be a Millionaire*, 55-minute programme at 20h05 on Sundays and at 22h00 on Fridays.
- Sports:
  - 30-minutes sports news slots at 14h30 on Mondays, Tuesdays, Wednesdays and Fridays;
  - *On the Pitch*: a 25-minute show at 22h00 on Mondays;
  - *Nigerian Football*: a 90-minute programme at 13h30 on Thursdays;
  - *Ultimate Sports Experience*: 10:30 to 11:00; Hotsports: 15h30 to 15h55; and *English Premiership* (live telecast) from 16h30 to 16h30 on Saturdays;
  - Nigerian football (live) from 16h00–18h00 on Sundays.
- Music shows (some examples):
  - *Trek Show*: one hour starting at 23h00 pm on Wednesdays;
  - *One Outing*: 06h00, 15 minutes; *Street Dance Africa* at 13h00 for one hour; *All Styles, All Ages* at 14h00 for 20 minutes on Saturdays;
  - *G-Bam Show*: 20h00 on weekdays for 30 minutes and 18h00 on Sundays (55 minutes).

2.2 Federal Radio Corporation of Nigeria (FRCN)

The FRCN's schedule consists of a mix of network programmes originated from headquarters and locally produced material. The network programmes which must be broadcast by all stations countrywide constitute about 40 per cent of overall weekly content.

Programme formats on the network schedule (all in English) include:

- News:
    - *Network News*, 07h00–08h00: news and a short commentary component
    - *Network Nigeria*, 12h00–13h00: news on rural/grassroots events from all the regions of the country (not on weekends)
    - *Network News*, 16h00–16h30: news from all parts of the country
    - *News in Brief*, 19h00–19h03: a short update on national events (not on weekends)
    - *Network News*, 22h00–22h30: national news
- Current affairs:
    - *From the FEC*, 19h03–19h30 on Wednesdays: covering the weekly meeting of the Federal Executive Council (the Cabinet). The programme relays the decisions of the council, puts them in context and points out policy trends emanating from them.
    - *Police Diary*, 08h30–09h00 on Tuesdays: featuring police officers who address crime issues, explaining activities of the police and answering phone-in questions and comments from members of the public.
    - *Senate This Week*, 14h30–15h00 on Thursdays: reporting events in the upper chamber of Parliament, the Senate, including interviews with members of the Senate.
    - *People's Representative*: similar to *Senate this Week*, covering the lower chamber of parliament, The House of Representatives.
    - *Radio Link*, 08h00– 10h00 on Saturdays: features discussions and interviews on current national issues, with in-studio participants and phone-ins.
    - *Consumer Speaks*, 08h30–09h00 on Wednesdays: talk programme designed to protect the rights of consumers. It usually features an official of the Consumer Protection Council who explains issues around consumer rights and reacts to phone-in contributions by the public.
    - *Health Watch*, 17h30–18h00: a resource person, usually a health sector practitioner, is interviewed on special topics, for example glaucoma. The programme aims to educate the public on good health practices.
- Drama: *Play of the Week*, 16h30–17h00 on Sundays: a local production on social issues.

- Sports: *Mid-week sports*, 17h30–18h00 on Wednesdays and *Sports Spectacular*, 17h30–18h00 on Sundays: feature developments on the sports scene with analysis and interviews. Additional slots through live broadcasts during matches or competitions involving Nigerian teams.

Programmes on the local stations appear to offer more variety in terms of format. Metro FM, for example, is one of the local FRCN stations in the Lagos area. The following are to be found on its schedule:

- Music: is the dominant format. It is given at least four slots daily and comes in various packages. For example:
    - *Spur the Tune*, 10h35–11h00 on Mondays, *VijuMilk Half Hour*, 11.30 am on Mondays and *Rock Music*, 17h00 on Thursdays: a mix of request music, talk and games.
    - *Music Studio*, 10h05–12h00 on Saturdays, *Café*, 14h05–16h00 on Saturdays, and *Chris Cruise*, 22h30 to midnight on Saturdays: all offering popular music.
- News: The station broadcasts news every hour. In addition to the bulletins provided by the network service it offers locally produced news bulletins lasting between two and five minutes at 06h00, 09h00, 10h00 and 11h00 as well as *City News* at 13h00 (10 minutes) and *Metro at Six News* at 18h00 (15 minutes).
- There are a number of current affairs and topical programmes:
    - *A M Lagos*, 08h00–08h30 and 09h00–09h30: a magazine programme with various components such as *Flashback*, a recap of major stories of the previous day *Make your Points*, which takes audience contributions on various national issues, and *Newspaper - Headlines*, a review of major stories in the daily newspapers circulated in the Lagos area.
    - *Political Train*, 11h05–11h30 on Mondays: a talk show on political events in the country. An anchor introduces and analyses an issue, and listeners contribute opinions.
    - *Streets of Lagos*, 15h15–15h30 on Mondays: voices and opinions of people on various issues affecting life in Lagos.
    - *I Beg Una*, 10h30–11h00 on Tuesdays: a Pidgin English phone-in programme that addresses anti-social behaviour.
    - *My Doctor and I*, 14h30–15h00 on Sundays: A health talk show in

which a resource person (expert) discusses a specific health topic (e.g diabetes), and answers questions posed by listeners.

- Sports:
  - *Metro Sports* or *Indomie Soccer Highlights*, 09h00–09h30 on Wednesdays and 11h30–11h45 on Saturdays: a review of major events of the previous days in the world of sports.
  - *Sport Summit*, 13h15–14h00 on Fridays: a talk show on current sports issues.
- Faith programmes:
  - *Purpose of High Calling*, 06h05–06h15 on weekdays: A Christian sermon
  - *Practical Christianity*, 06h40–06h50 on Saturdays.
  - Various other religious programmes are broadcast between 07h00 and 11h00 on Sundays.
  - *Hymns of Praise*, 22h35–23h15 on Sundays: Christian hymns as requested by listeners.

3   Programming of non-state broadcasters

3.1   Television

Africa Independent Television (AIT) in Lagos is one of the most popular out of the 14 free-to-air stations in the country. It is on-air around the clock and offers a variety of programmes.

- News:
  - *AIT Reports*, 11h30–12h30: national news
  - *World News*, 16h00–16h20: national and international news
  - *AIT News*, 18h30–18h25: national news
  - *Newshour*, 20h00–21h00: local and foreign news
  - *AIT News*, at midnight, a 30-minute package of local news.
- Magazine: *Kaakaki*, from 06h00–09h00 on weekdays: The programme has components such as reviews of headlines of major national newspapers, sports, interviews and local news.
- Current affairs (examples):
  - *Focus Nigeria*, 09h30–10h30 on weekdays: a talk show

with interviews and discussions on contemporary issues of national interest. Occasionally the programme includes short documentaries or feature clips on the activities of state government agencies.

– *Democratic Licence*, 17h00–18h00 Mondays: features interviews and discussions on governance issues of national interest.

– *The Money Show*, 10h30–11h30 on weekdays: The programme begins with headline news on major events in the economic sector, goes on to interview an expert on a chosen topic in the sector, and offers analysis on the stock market.

• Drama: Up to three slots of between 20 and 25 minutes a day, mainly soap operas.
• Documentaries: at least one slot a day.
• Quiz/games:
    – *Family Game Show*, 19h00–19h50 on Wednesdays
    – *Panadol Extra Kampe*, 16h30–16h55 on Saturdays
• Sports:
    – *Sports Extra*, a slot in the daily Kaakaki magazine
    – *Sport Today*, 14h00–14h25 on Mondays and Wednesdays
    – *Sport File*, 13h00–14h00 on Saturdays.
• Music: Examples are *Music Television Base* (weekdays 18h00–18h25), *My Playlist* (22h30–22h50 on Mondays), *Ten Street Beatz* (22h30–22h55 on Tuesdays), *Gbedu* (13h30–14h00 on Thursdays) and *Sound City* (23h05–23h30 pm on Fridays).
• Faith programmes (examples):
    – *A Light for the Nation*, 05h45–06h00 throughout the week: Christian preaching programme
    – *Christ Embassy*, 18h00–18h25 on Saturdays
    – *The Hour of Salvation*, 19h00–19h30 on Sundays
    – *Catholic Holy Mass*, 08h00–10h00 on Sundays.

3.2 Radio

Raypower 100.5 FM, the radio station with the largest audience in Lagos, is predominantly an entertainment station, with over 60 per cent of its 24-hour schedule dedicated to music.

• Music programmes feature most prominently from late morning to late at night:

- *Sunnyside Up*, 10h15–12h00: uninterrupted popular music
- *Lunchtime*, 12h15–14h00
- *Primetime Africa*, 14h00–15h30 and 16h30–17h00: a mix of music, talk, games and information
- *Power play*, 18h30–18h45, 19h00–20h00 and 20h05–21h00
- *Soul Serenade*, 21h00–24h00: cool bedtime music
- *Quiet storm*, 24h00–05h00.

- News: Bulletins are offered every two hours on average, lasting between four and 25 minutes. These include:
  - *Nigeria This Morning*, 06h00–06h05: a bulletin which recaps the stories of the previous day
  - *Global News*, 07h00–07h15
  - *Biz Update*, 07h45–08h00: a business news digest
  - *News @ 10*, 10h00–10h15
  - *News @ 12*, 12h00–12h15
  - *Window on Africa*, 16h00–16h30: a continental bulletin
  - *Nigeria Today*, 18h00–18h30, a national bulletin
  - *News flakes*, 20h00–20h05, a local bulletin.

All these news bulletins run on weekdays. Only a few – *News @ 10*, *News @12* and *Nigeria Today* – are aired over the weekend.

- Magazines: The prime example is the *Ultimate Morning Show*, which runs (sandwiched between other programmes) from 05h00 to 05h20, 05h30 to 06h00, 06h05 to 07h00, 07h30 to 07h45, 09h00 to 09h05 and 09h30 to 10h00.
- Current Affairs (examples):
  - *Fact file*, 08h25–09h00 on weekdays: a talk programme
  - *Political Platform*, 09h15–09h45: talk show with guests in the studio and phone-ins
  - *Vision Nigeria*, 13h05–14h00 on Wednesdays: a talk programme which focuses on challenges facing the country; it features a guest speaker and takes phone-in contributions from listeners.
- Indigenous language programmes: There are three programmes in the country's major languages and one in one of the minority languages of the Niger Delta region. *Mimi Jojo*, the Yoruba language programme, runs for 105 minutes at 10h15 on Tuesdays, and *Yakpotuba* (Igbo language) and *Dada Ido* (Hausa) in the same time slot on Thursdays and Fridays respectively.

A one-hour Request Show at 13h00 on Sundays is broadcast in the Afemai language.

- Sports: There is an average of five daily sports programmes on the station, for example *BBC Sports* (relay from the BBC World Service) from 05h20 to 05h50 daily, *Milo World of Sports* (07h15–07h30), *Peak Soccer Moment* (08h00–08h15), *Fast Track* (17h30–18h00), another relay from the BBC World Service, and *Sport Round Up* (18h45–19h00).

- Faith programmes: There are a number of such programmes, particularly on Sundays. These include *Apokalypsis*, a Christian preaching programme (07h00–07h20), *Living Truth* (07h45–08h00), and *When God and I Talk* (08h00–08h30).

4   News and current affairs

4.1   State broadcasters

Nigerian Television Authority (NTA)

The main bulletin of NTA, *Network News* at 21h00 is dominated by news from government agencies, accounting for over 90 per cent. The structure follows a standard pattern: news from the Presidency comes first, then the federal legislature, followed by the ministries, state governments and so on. This order may change on weekends. Stories from, say, the Federal House of Representatives may come early in the bulletin if there are no Presidency items due to the lack of reported official engagements there.

The news bulletin also covers other sectors of public life such as agriculture, education, transportation, power supply or health, again with the focus being mostly on government activities. Non-government news sources often feature as secondary sources.

The few non-government stories in the bulletins usually come in sponsored segments such as Business News, Small and Medium Enterprises (SME) Updates or Sports. On Fridays and Sundays, religious news items (Mosque and Church) also feature.

Among NTA's prominent current affairs programmes is *Tuesday Live*, broadcast for two hours in the late evening from 23h00 to 01h00. In the show, a topic of current interest is tackled by a panel of discussants in the studio, an in-studio audience and phone-in participation from viewers. Participants come from both government and non-government sectors. One recent edition on 'The Media in Building a Sustainable

Democracy', for example, featured a former Information Minister, a current member of parliament and a media scholar, as well as a professor of mass communication as panelists.

Federal Radio Corporation of Nigeria (FRCN)

Among FRCN's major news programmes is *Network News* at 07h00, a one-hour show which covers all sectors of public life: health, economy, politics, agriculture, education, etc.

News on government activities and from government agencies dominate, accounting for over 90 per cent. Even where an event is organised by a non-government body, the news is given a government angle, most commonly by treating the statement made by the government official at the event as more newsworthy than the others.

The sequencing follows the same standard pattern as NTA's news: stories from the Presidency come first, then the federal legislature, followed by the ministries, state governments and so on.

The few non-government stories could be on media industry unions or the ruling People Democratic Party. The opposition rarely gets news coverage on this network.

Business and financial news, presented in a dedicated segment, sometimes contain stories on labour unions especially when they speak at events on business activities.

Special Reports also provide some opportunity for non-government voices to be heard. In one recent example, a report covering the debate on the retention or otherwise of the present national anthem featured voices of ordinary citizens.

A popular current affairs programme is *Radio Link*. Aired on Saturdays from 08h00 to 10h00, it features discussions and interviews on current national issues, with in-studio participants and public contributions fed in through phone-ins from various parts of the country. A recent edition dealt with the state of football development in the country. Other subjects discussed included "How to wipe out tuberculosis (TB) in the country' and 'How the country should respond to Climate Change'. The selection of discussants on this programme usually shows some diversity, featuring representatives of government, independent practitioners in the sector and people with first-hand knowledge on the subject concerned, for example a former TB patient in the edition on TB aired on 27 March, 2010.

4.2 Non-state broadcasters

Television

In Africa Independent Television's (AIT) main bulletin *Newshour* at 20h00, stories which emanate from government usually outnumber those from other sources and follow-up stories on government announcements or policies are prioritised. Voices of ordinary people are given space when public reaction to government policies is being sought.

Business news are packaged in a special (sponsored) segment and stories could be government or non-government related, local or international.

Focus Nigeria (21h30–22h30am on weekdays) – a panel discussion moderated by an anchor – is one of the station's major current affairs programmes. Panelists are usually selected from various backgrounds. One edition featured the post-amnesty programme of the government in the Niger Delta. After militants had surrendered arms, the government embarked on a resettlement drive and attempted to address what were seen as the root causes that had led to the militancy. The discussion featured representatives from civil society organisations based in the Niger Delta region. Another programme focused on the planned deregulation of the Nigerian petroleum industry and the possible price inflation expected to result from it. A private financial analyst was the interviewee. From time to time, sponsored documentaries produced by government agencies to showcase their activities to the public are broadcast in this slot. One recent edition featured a documentary on the achievement of the government of Jigawa State, in the north-west region of the country.

Radio

More than 90 per cent of items covered in the major news bulletin of Raypower FM, *Nigeria Today*, are stories on government activities and from government agencies. The difference in structure from the bulletins of the state broadcaster is that *Nigeria Today* does not follow the hierarchical order as laid down by government protocol. The leading items in the bulletin could be from state governments or parastatals. The few non-government related items are accommodated under the business or sports segments.

Fact file is one of the more prominent current affairs discussion programmes on this station. Usually the presenter introduces an issue, puts it in context and invites listeners' opinions through phone-ins. Sometimes an expert is invited as a studio guest, either from government or from any other sector of society. Listeners also call in from diverse locations and with diverse backgrounds. Among some recent topics covered on this programme were the planned deregulation of the oil sector, the (mis)management of the Ecological Fund by state governors, and bail conditions for accused persons set by Nigerian law courts.

Another edition of *Fact file* addressed the question whether, in view of the demands of the Electoral Commission for an amount of N 72 billion (US$ 480 million) to prepare a new voters register and the time available for the exercise, Nigeria should make do with the old register or have a new one compiled. The majority of the listeners who contributed to the discussion (some sent sms messages) wanted a new voters' register compiled. The main arguments were that the old one, if used, would lead to a flawed election, and that if the funds were not used for this purpose, they might be misappropriated by political office holders. A minority argued that the money could be put to better use if deployed to developing public infrastructure such as power supply and road transportation.

Political Platform is another talk show on Raypower FM which tackles current national political issues, with a main anchor, a studio-based team and listeners' opinions being sent in by text (sms) messages and read out by the anchor. One edition monitored, for example, addressed a number of thorny issues: the intention of state governors to take a common position on the adoption of a plan to divide the country into zones for the election of candidates into the office of President; the pros and cons of the new countrywide voter registration exercise as suggested by the electoral body; and how best to tackle vote-rigging in the upcoming elections in view of the revelations made at an Abuja forum by a former state governor on the tactics used by state chief executives to rig elections across the country in the past.

5   Feedback and complaints procedures

There are no organised feedback or complaints mechanisms in place at any of the country's state or private broadcasters. All broadcasting organisations rely mainly on comments by the audience during phone-in programmes and opinions expressed in the print media. These data are not collated and examined in context.

6   Funding of public interest programming of private broadcasters

Public interest programming on private/commercial stations is mainly funded by revenue generated from advertisements or sponsorship of other types of programmes. The proportion of overall expenditure which goes into funding public interest programming is not made public.

Government agencies seldom sponsor public interest programmes except for the purpose of image-laundering. Examples are *Living Spring and Development Today*, programmes on MITV paid for by the Osun and Ogun state governments respectively. They are usually packaged by outside producers and present only positive opinions about the sponsoring government agencies, without any input from professionals at the station. Private broadcasters accept and air them (as long as they do not break any laws) because of the money they bring in.

International donor and development agencies prefer to support the training of staff rather than providing funding for programmes. An agency like UNICEF sometimes organises training workshops for broadcasters on programming for and coverage of children's issues.

The private (business) sector sponsors business-oriented drama or sports programmes.

7   Conclusions and recommendations

The two state broadcasters, NTA and FRCN, offer a variety of programme formats through which they disseminate a large amount of content to their audiences. Also common to both is the split between network programming provided for all alike from headquarters and the individual station services.

News occupies prime space on the schedules of these broadcasters, but bulletins give voice almost exclusively to government spokespersons, members or agencies. In other programme genres where the voices of citizens are heard, access is limited. Companies or organisations who buy airtime to flight programmes will select only those voices that suit their goals.

News in commercial stations is also dominated by stories on government activities. Access to commercial broadcasters is limited because their programming is mainly in English rather than the various indigenous languages. Music and other forms of entertainment are kings on commercial broadcasting stations, neglecting the numerous development challenges in Nigeria.

Recommendations

- The essential precondition for any reform of programming on the NTA and FRCN is the transformation of these state broadcasters into genuinely public broadcasters. On this basis:

    - the overall programming of both organisations must be reviewed in a thorough public consultation process;
    - news and current affairs programming must offer a platform for democratic information and debate which does not serve government agencies only but the public at large;

- – in-house guidelines and policies should be developed, publicised and enforced, including an effective internal complaints mechanism through which citizens can express their concerns about content they find inappropriate.
- Commercial broadcasters should:
  - – re-orientate their programming, in particular on radio, to cater for the broader needs of the public;
  - – introduce more programming in indigenous languages and more public interest programmes;
  - – be assisted in achieving these goals by government and corporate bodies which should sponsor more of such programmes (without interfering in the editorial independence of these broadcasters).
- The proportions of local and foreign content stipulated in regulation should be enforced in the programming of all broadcasting organisations.
- Independent producers should be encouraged to be more creative and promote Nigeria's cultural values in content development.
- Stakeholders (e.g. regulator, broadcasters, educational institutions) should strengthen the collaboration between newsroom and classroom for content enrichment, skills development and feedback.
- Management and infrastructure of the training arm of the broadcast industry should be updated and maintained.

9
Broadcasting Reform Efforts

There appears to be consensus among civil society groups and their representatives in Nigeria[72] that neither the Nigerian Television Authority (NTA) nor the Federal Radio Corporation of Nigeria (FRCN) are truly public broadcasters. The main points of criticism are that both organisations

- protect government's interests under the guise of protecting the 'national interest';
- spend an inordinate amount of time on covering government activities and portraying government in a good light while denying the people access;
- are public broadcast organisations in theory, but in practice do not serve the public good;
- are government media that convey things the way the authorities want them to be seen;
- are perpetually pro-government and sometimes unprofessional.

Respondents agree that control of the two broadcasters is presently in the hands of the federal government through the information ministry and the presidency. This, they say, is evidenced by the existence of ministerial interference in the broadcasters' operations, the appointment of their governing organs (board and management) by government, their overwhelmingly pro-government programming, and the fact that they are fully owned, supervised and maintained by government.

A number of alternative solutions for bodies to supervise the broadcasters are suggested: a board of trustees composed of various sections of the public such as government, parliament, labour and civil society; the national parliament as the elected

---

72 Interviews conducted in May/June 2008 with, among many others, Henry Odugala, General Secretary of Radio, Television, Theatre and Allied Workers Union (RATTAWU), Abuja; Owei Lakemfa, Spokesman of the Nigeria Labour Congress (NLC), Abuja; and Lanre Arogundade, Coordinator, International Press Centre (IPC), Lagos.

representatives of the people; an independent National Broadcasting Commission; a new, converged regulatory body that would have regulatory control over both broadcasting and telecommunications; or a body made up solely of representatives of civil society organisations.

A majority of the responses favour a role for parliament in governance of the public broadcasters. Parliament should review existing broadcasting laws described as 'archaic' and carry out oversight functions, while the governing organs of these organisations should be accountable to the parliament.

There is also consensus that civil society should play a major role in regard to public broadcasting. Three key components of that role are suggested: representation on the governing organs of the broadcasters; monitoring of programming to ensure compliance with standards and regulations, access to the poor and provision of an inclusive platform; and carrying out advocacy for pro-people public broadcasting.

1   Previous reform efforts

Efforts to reform broadcasting and other media have been on the public agenda since Nigeria's return to civil rule in 1999 and include a number of initiatives:

- A Freedom of Information (FOI) Bill was introduced in the lower house of parliament, the House of Representatives, in 1999. The bill sought (and seeks) to grant the public, including broadcast media, access to government-held information. The advocates and facilitators of the bill, led by Media Rights Agenda (MRA), a civil society group, explained that it was meant to 'eliminate unnecessary secrecy in the conduct of public affairs and inject the virtue of transparency and accountability into the governance process so as to promote the social, political and economic growth of the nation'. In the specific case of the media, they said that the bill would enable journalists to perform their constitutionally assigned duty to 'uphold the responsibility and accountability of the government to the people'. Despite vigorous advocacy for the bill, it had not been adopted by the time the tenure of that parliament ended in 2003.
  Re-presented in 2003 it was passed by the new parliament in its final days in 2007. However, the president refused to assent and sign it into law, and the document got stuck in the tangles of government bureaucracy. The bill started its journey for the third time in 2007 when it was introduced afresh in the new parliament. At the time of writing it was still being separately considered by the two chambers.

- Also in 1999, another civil society organisation, Centre for Free Speech (CFS), sought legal reform in broadcasting, as well as in the broader media and freedom of expression landscape. It drew up a bill to effect the repeal of laws it considered anti-media, the protection of journalists' sources of information, guarantees of citizens' rights to criticise government officials and institutions, and liberalisation of the broadcast industry, among others. The bill was not taken up by parliament, and it has not been re-presented.

- A 'Nigerian Media Bill', presented to parliament in 2001, sought to harmonise and introduce innovations to existing media laws in the country. In the specific case of broadcasting, it introduced a framework which recognises and provides for three different sub-sectors of broadcasting – public, commercial and community. The bill had not been addressed when parliament wound down in 2003. Its sponsor, Media Rights Agenda (MRA), has not re-presented it.

- The Nigeria Union of Journalists (NUJ), the central professional body of journalists in the country, drew up a 'Journalism Practice Enhancement Bill' for consideration by the House of Representatives in 2002. The document focused on such issues as working conditions of journalists, requirements for the establishment of media organisations and entry qualifications for the profession, but became mired in internal controversy. Strong and influential voices within the ranks of the NUJ insisted that the envisaged provisions would shackle rather than enhance journalism practice. The House stopped consideration of the bill.

- A reform effort targeting the development of community broadcasting and broadcasting pluralism began to take shape in 2003. The 'Initiative on Building Community Radio Broadcasting in Nigeria' was launched by a partnership between the Institute for Media and Society (IMS), a local civil society organisation, and two international CSOs – the Panos Institute West Africa (PIWA) and the World Association of Community Radio Broadcasters (AMARC). The initiative put in place an advocacy programme in the form of country-wide awareness and strategy workshops involving academia, professional groups and international development agencies. This has resulted in broad-based participation and support for the aim of community broadcasting. Membership stands at 250 institutions and individuals and the initiative has established an umbrella body, the Nigeria Community Radio Coalition. In the second leg of its strategy, issues of policy, legal and regulatory reforms are being addressed. In its flagship advocacy document, 'Roadmap to Building a Sustainable Community Radio Sector in Nigeria: The Stakeholders' Charter', the initiative outlines the history and current status of the country's radio broadcasting landscape, and makes demands for reforms in policy, legislation and regulation.

- The initiative proposes that a total of 19 existing laws (which it says are inimical to media development) be repealed, that others (including the NBC Act and the country's Constitution) be reviewed, that one (the FOI Bill) be passed, and that some international instruments be domesticated and incorporated in national law.

The government, for its part, has also undertaken some broadcasting reform efforts – although these are largely seen as a response to the advocacy of civil society groups. Such efforts include the following:

- In 2001, the government submitted a bill seeking a review of the NBC Act 38 (as amended by Act 55) to parliament. It was not passed by the end of that legislative term in 2003. Government has not re-presented it.
- In the same year, the government set up a committee to examine the feasibility of a Mass Media Trust Fund, which would provide independent funding for its radio and television stations. But the effort died quietly because the information minister who had inaugurated the committee was removed from office before it had completed its assignment. His successors showed no interest.
- In 2002, another working group was set up by government to review the laws establishing the parastatals supervised by the information ministry. Among these parastatals are the Nigerian Television Authority and the Federal Radio Corporation of Nigeria. The intention was to present the review document as a bill to parliament. The working group completed its assignment but government did not submit a bill.
- A working group to review the 1990 National Mass Communication Policy was instituted by the government in 2004. The group completed its assignment and submitted a report to government in December of that year. A final policy document has yet to be issued to the public.
- In 2006, a 17-member working group was established by government to draw up a National Community Radio Policy. The report submitted by the group was considered and ratified by the National Council on Information, the government's policy organ. But no final document has been published.
- Also in 2006, another working group was instituted to design a National Frequency Spectrum Management Policy. Government's final word on the report that emerged from that process is still being awaited by the public.

- In November 2009, the federal government and UNICEF organised a
  conference to review the Mass Communication Policy and the Community
  Radio Policy. The information minister said at the time that the government
  wanted to take these policy processes to conclusion.

The story of broadcasting sector reform over the last decade is thus not that of an
absence or dearth of efforts, but rather of numerous attempts by civil society and
government which usually begin on a bright note, then get caught in bureaucratic and
political webs, and finally peter out and come to nothing.

There are various explanations for this.

First, interest in and commitment to broadcasting reforms vary among the different
government agencies. For example, while policy documents are getting stalled on
the information ministry/presidency level and bills are not finalised and passed in
parliament, the National Broadcasting Commission has ensured a regular three-yearly
review of its Nigerian Broadcasting Code. Each review has produced improvements on
earlier editions.

Second, there is a huge turnover of key officials and lack of continuity in
government agencies. In the years of civil rule since 1999 there have been seven
information ministers. An initiative begun under one minister does not usually
receive favourable and urgent attention by his successor even though they serve in the
same government.

Inconsistency has also been a feature of governance in the information sector.
In early 2007, the government approved licences for radio stations on campuses
of universities and polytechnics which the regulatory body began to categorise as
community broadcasting licences. But the plan announced by the government when
it set up the working group on Community Radio Policy was that it wanted grassroots/
rural community radio stations and that a policy would precede the licensing.

2   Current reform efforts

There is currently no structured debate on media reforms, including the future of
public broadcasting in Nigeria. Representatives of the leadership of the NTA and
FRCN, as well as from academia and civil society, have raised a number of issues.

For example Eddie Iroh, former director-general of the FRCN, has advocated a
transition of the state broadcaster to a public broadcaster, giving indigenous languages
greater prominence in the medium, and the need for community broadcasting. He has
also recommended a funding arrangement for public broadcasters which would entail

provision of 50 per cent of revenue from a statutory parliament-appropriated budget, and 50 per cent from commercial advertising – excluding all forms of 'sponsorship' – with loans to be sourced from the capital market in the event of a shortfall.[73]

The former director-general at the NTA, Tonnie Iredia, has made suggestions which include:

- The amendment of enabling (i.e. establishing) laws of the state broadcasters to remove/streamline the wide powers of information ministers to give directions of a general nature, making chief executive officers of the broadcasters independent and appointable by the president after parliamentary ratification, taking the broadcasters out of the civil service structure and giving them autonomy to fix their salaries and remunerations and retain their internally generated revenue;
- The enforcement of broadcasting guidelines by the NBC to ensure standardisation (of rules for the operations of state and other broadcasters);
- The standardisation of working conditions, remuneration and emoluments of workers in the broadcasting industry;
- An improvement of the infrastructural base for broadcasting.[74]

Academics have also made important contributions. For instance, in a 2007 study on radio in Nigeria, authors Ojebode and Adegbola (lecturer in communication arts at the University of Ibadan and head of the African Languages Technology Initiative, Ibadan, respectively) recommended that government:

- Should take its hands off the ownership and management of radio broadcasting, and allow a truly public service broadcasting system to be put in place;
- Should allow the establishment of community radio, so that radio will engage development more fruitfully;
- Must support private commercial stations for them to fruitfully participate in development communication.[75]

Generally, it must be observed that the intellectual output in regard to media issues in Nigeria is rather scanty, a reality which has affected the country for some time.

---

73   See Eddie Iroh, 'An examination of the funding model for broadcasting in the West African sub-region', *The Guardian* (of Lagos), 3 May 2006.
74   See T. Iredia, 'Broadcasting in a developing country: challenges to professionalism', *The Daily Independent*, 3–7 September 2007.
75   See A. Ojebode and T. Adegbola, *Engaging Development: Environment and Content of Radio Broadcasting in Nigeria*, 2007, pp. 58–59.

3   Conclusions and recommendations

The desire for reform of the broadcasting sector is alive in Nigeria. However, there are two main challenges: One is the lack of coordination among stakeholders. The other is lethargy in government.

So far; each stakeholder group has pushed its own side of reform advocacy while government takes steps that never produce concrete results.

Recommendations

Civil society groups engaged in media issues, broadcasting in particular, should form a working group to assess their reform objectives and strategies with the aim to form a coalition to push effectively for broadcasting reform. Priority should be given to:

- Developing a common policy document which sets out the objectives of reform;
- Initiating public debate on broadcasting issues throughout the country;
- Involving other civil society groups such as faith organisations, trade unions and human rights organisations in their campaigns;
- Lobbying parliament, especially its relevant committees and legislators who care about human rights and good governance, on the essentials of democratic broadcasting reform;
- Continuing dialogue with the executive branch of government (especially the ministry of information and communication) to ensure the full adoption of proposed reforms.

10
Overall Conclusions and Recommendations

About 50 years after political independence, legislation constricting media freedom and freedom of expression which dates from colonial times remains on the statute books and new laws are being enacted which retain the culture of harshness. These legal instruments have been used extensively by government authorities throughout the period of post-independence governance under military and civilian rulers.

Many of these laws are in contravention of the Declaration of Principles on Freedom of Expression in Africa, which provides for the right of freedom of expression and information.

Nigeria's liberalisation journey in the broadcasting sector has gone only half-way, concentrating almost exclusively on commercial broadcasting. This is not in line with both the letter and spirit of the Declaration, which provides for the encouragement of a diverse, independent broadcasting sector, including the promotion of community broadcasting.

A particular source of concern is whether Nigeria will meet the 2015 deadline set by the International Telecommunications Union (ITU). The delay in policy development and implementation gives the impression that there is insufficient political will and commitment by government.

The legislation, regulatory structure and culture in place in the field of broadcasting are a vestige of military rule. The regulator, the National Broadcasting Commission (NBC), lacks independence and adequate protection against political and economic interference and is accountable to the executive arm of government.

Broadcasting licensing procedures are shrouded in secrecy and the granting of licences is left to the discretion of the president.

Neither the Federal Radio Corporation of Nigeria (FRCN) nor the Nigerian Television Authority (NTA) can be described as public broadcasters as defined by the

Declaration of Principles on Freedom of Expression in Africa, which says that such broadcasters should be accountable to the public through the legislature rather than the executive arm of government.

From their founding legislation, through the administrative structures and running of the organisations, to the service conditions and general welfare of their personnel, both the FRCN and NTA are clearly positioned as state broadcasters. A governing body appointed at the pleasure of government officials through processes that lack transparency can only be loyal to the government, not the people. An organisation subject to government interference prescribed in law can only be the voice of government. A structure immersed in the constricting civil service culture cannot compete in the professional broadcasting world of the 21st century.

The two main sources of income for the state broadcasters – government grants and advertisements/sponsorships – also do not comply with the Declaration of Principles on Freedom of Expression in Africa, which says that 'public broadcasters should be adequately funded in a manner that protects them from arbitrary interference with their budgets'.

Due to the unpredictability and inadequacy of grants from government, sufficient resources are not available for activities at the appropriate times. In their desperation to shore up revenues through the market, the organisations end up ceding editorial control to business and other interests with the money to buy and influence programming.

Despite these constraints, the two state broadcasters have a wide spectrum of programme formats through which they disseminate a large amount of content to their audiences.

The news bulletins of the FRCN and NTA virtually give voice only to government representatives, spokespersons and agencies. On other programme genres where the voices of citizens are heard, access is limited. Companies or organisations who buy airtime for their programmes will select only those voices that suit their goals.

Access to commercial broadcasters is also limited because their programming is mainly in English and they do not communicate in the various indigenous languages. Music and other forms of entertainment dominate their schedules, while the numerous development challenges in Nigeria are largely ignored.

The desire for reform of the broadcasting sector is alive in Nigeria but faces two main challenges: One is the lack of coordination among stakeholders to produce synergies and speed in the efforts. The other is lack of political will on the part of the government. So far, each stakeholder group has pushed its side of reform advocacy only while government takes tentative and half-hearted steps that are never brought to conclusion.

Recommendations

Media legislation and regulation

- The following pieces of legislation should be repealed in their entirety:
  - The Nigerian Press Council Act;
  - Legislation on sedition – sections 50–52 of the Criminal Code and section 416 of the Penal Code;
  - Legislation on criminal defamation – sections 373–379 of the Criminal Code and sections 391-395 of the Penal Code;
  - The Official Secrets Act;
  - The Offensive Publications Decree 35 of 1993;
  - The Printing Presses Regulation Act;
  - The Newspaper Act and Newspaper Amendment Act.
- Laws to regulate the media should respect the principles of international human rights standards, including the International Covenant on Civil and Political Rights (ICCPR), African Charter on Human and Peoples' Rights and the Declaration of Principles on Freedom of Expression in Africa.
- The Freedom of Information Bill currently before the National Assembly should be passed into law only after a process of full public consultation to make sure that the final legislation is agreed to by civil society and other stakeholders. The Act should ensure that, among other things, access to information is granted by the state body in possession of the information sought, and that courts of law serve only as appeal mechanisms.
- An independent Press Council should be established to promote media self-regulation, enhance professional journalistic standards and serve as a complaints body for the public.

The broadcasting landscape

- The government should complete all the policy processes it initiated – regarding a National Mass Communication Policy, National Frequency Management Policy, and National Community Radio Policy – and embark on legal reform. It should work in consultation with advocacy groups to ensure that the draft policies comply with accepted international democratic standards.
- Industry stakeholders, including the regulatory agency, should address the issue of possible cooperative management of transmission and standardisation

of equipment. This is particularly important now in the era of digitalisation, with different technologies offered by developed countries.

- The NBC should begin to license rural, suburban and urban community broadcasting stations, including campus radios.
- Licence fees for commercial broadcasters should be reduced while community broadcasters should get their licences for free or a nominal amount. Annual charges should be suspended until an independent regulator is in place, the economic/business environment of broadcasting improves, and stakeholders agree on the amount to be charged.
- To prevent concentration in the media industry, one person or body should not be allowed to have controlling shares in more than one radio and one TV station simultaneously.
- The NBC, training/research and other institutions should conduct studies on such subjects as technical coverage of the country, and audience research.
- Technical quality standards should be reinforced and more widely adopted.

Digitalisation

- The federal government should speedily translate the report of the presidential advisory committee on digitalisation into public policy, organise public consultations, invite public input, issue its white paper and give implementation directives.
- The existing broadcasting law and regulation should be reviewed to incorporate issues of broadcasting digitalisation.
- The National Population Commission should release data gathered on TV/radio-set ownership from the last population and household census, so that this information will be available for broadcasting policies and planning.
- The National Broadcasting Commission (NBC) should be empowered to conduct surveys and update the data gathered on TV/radio-set ownership during the last census.
- The NBC should continue to create awareness about the importance and challenges of digitalisation.

Broadcasting legislation and regulation

- An updated broadcasting policy should be put in place. This should include the completion of the review process of the 1990 National Mass Communication Policy and updating of the broadcasting policy contained in that document, also taking into account the 2004 National Mass Communication Policy review draft and the 2006 Community Radio Policy Document.

- Section 39(2) of the country's Constitution, which gives the president power to authorise broadcasting licences, should be amended, such that this power will vest in the regulatory body.
- The NBC Act should be reviewed and deliver the following:
  - A converged regulatory body which should be independent and have an administrative structure designed in a way that will allow for equitable attention to all the subsectors, including broadcasting.
  - The regulatory body should be independent of the government, political parties and media interests.
  - Its members should be appointed by parliament in a transparent and public process which involves consultation with civil society and other specific constituencies from which the members are drawn. Government agencies, political parties and persons with financial interests in the industry should be disqualified from membership. Members of the NBC should be granted security of tenure.
  - The NBC should be vested with full regulatory powers, including the power to process applications and grant licences, without reference to government organs like the ministry of information and the presidency.
  - The NBC should be accountable to the public through parliament.
  - It should be funded through direct budgetary allocation from parliament as well as from a share of radio/TV-set licence fees.
  - The licensing process should be transparent. Clear criteria and procedure for licensing, agreed upon in consultation with stakeholders, should be advertised by the NBC. Time limits should be set for the process, explanations should be supplied to unsuccessful applicants, and there should be provision for appeals through institutions such as the courts.
  - Political parties and owners of other media, particularly newspapers, should be ineligible for obtaining a broadcasting licence.
  - Religious organisations should be eligible for broadcasting

licences subject to criteria such as: restriction of coverage to geographical and homogenous communities; a commitment to devote a substantial proportion of their airtime to secular public interest programming; and an undertaking that their content will not offend religious, ethnic and other sensibilities.

- Precise proportional stipulations of local and foreign content of broadcasters' programming should be removed from legislation and left for the consideration of the NBC in consultation with stakeholders.
- The complaints and sanctions process should be reviewed to guarantee:
  » an appeals mechanism – through the establishment of either a broadcasting complaints body or a special, higher-level body within the regulator, as well as the courts;
  » an industry consultative mechanism to undertake a periodic review of the proportionality of stations' offences to imposed sanctions.

- All the above reviews should be done with the participation of stakeholders and civil society at large.
- The on-going process of licensing private commercial broadcasting networks should be concluded and the federal government should, through the NBC, announce the results of the 2009 bid process.

State broadcasters – legislation and regulation

- Existing legislation for the two state broadcasters – the NTA Act 24 of 1977 and FRCN Act of 1979 (with its amendments) – should be replaced by a new act establishing Radio and Television Nigeria as genuine public service broadcasters.
- The new legislation should be developed through a broad consultation process with the participation of all interested stakeholders and the public at large.
- The new legislation should establish the public broadcaster as an independent legal entity with editorial independence and strong safeguards against any interference from the federal government, state governments and other interests.
- The public broadcaster should be governed by a board established and acting according to the following principles:

- appointment procedures should be open, transparent and free from political interference;
- the board should represent a broad cross-section of the Nigerian population;
- its role should be clearly set out in law and its main responsibility should be to ensure that the public broadcaster fulfils its mandate in the public interest and is protected against undue political or commercial influences;
- the board should not interfere in the day-to-day decision-making of the broadcaster, especially in relation to broadcast content, and respect the principle of editorial independence.
- Even prior to the enactment of new legislation and the setting up of a new board the following priorities should be given urgent attention:
  - commercial and editorial decisions should be separated to prevent conflict of interest, and the practice of accepting 'news' paid for by institutions, business, government or others should be stopped;
  - the directorate of news should be enabled to take autonomous decisions. Its director should be the editor-in-chief, whose judgments will be based on criteria of newsworthiness and not on commercial considerations;
  - an audit of organisational structures should be undertaken with the aim of discarding inappropriate and inflexible civil service hierarchies and conditions of service (including salaries) and turning the corporation(s) into modern broadcasters able to compete in a fast changing media environment.

Funding of state broadcasters

- The entire system of funding for the NTA and FRCN needs to be thoroughly reviewed to guarantee their financial independence. To this end:
  - the corporations' financial status (sources of income and spending) should be examined by an independent accounting firm and be opened up to public scrutiny;
  - programme policies must be revisited and the broadcasters must assume full and exclusive editorial control over news and current affairs in particular;
  - on the basis of new programme policies and new organisational

structures designed to implement them, business plans must be developed which reflect the financial needs of the NTA and FRCN and potential sources of revenue.

- The NTA and FRCN should derive their funding from a mix of broadcast licence fees, government grants and (to a limited extent) advertisements.
- Regarding licence fees it is recommended that:
  - the collecting agencies should be the government revenue agencies. The overall licence fee revenue will go to the National Broadcasting Commission for distribution to broadcasters in the public, commercial and community subsectors;
  - fee amounts should be is set in a way that allows for stable, predictable multi-year funding, enabling the broadcasters to plan and implement the necessary investment in programming and operational improvements.
- In regard to revenues from the state treasury it is recommended that:
  - an independent panel of experts determine the amount of subsidies needed by the NTA and FRCN over a three-year period to fulfill their public broadcasting mandate;
  - the National Assembly fund the public broadcasters directly (and not through a ministry or department) on the basis of the amount determined by the panel of experts, with the monies to be disbursed annually.
- Concerning advertisements and sponsorships it is recommended that:
  - The NTA and FRCN develop clear and strict guidelines on soliciting advertisements and conditions for accepting advertisements and programme sponsorships that will safeguard the broadcasters' editorial independence;
  - the broadcasting regulator embark on a process of public consultation with the objective to set appropriate limits to advertising and sponsorship on the NTA and FRCN.

Programming

- The essential precondition for any reform of programming on the NTA and FRCN is the transformation of these state broadcasters into genuinely public broadcasters. On this basis:
  - the overall programming of both organisations must be reviewed in a thorough public consultation process;

- news and current affairs programming must offer a platform for democratic information and debate which does not serve government agencies only but the public at large;
- in-house guidelines and policies should be developed, publicised and enforced, including an effective internal complaints mechanism through which citizens can express their concerns about content they find inappropriate.
- Commercial broadcasters should:
  - re-orientate their programming, in particular on radio, to cater for the broader needs of the public;
  - introduce more programming in indigenous languages and more public interest programmes;
  - be assisted in achieving these goals by government and corporate bodies, which should sponsor more of such programmes (without interfering in the editorial independence of these broadcasters).
- The proportions of local and foreign content stipulated in regulation should be enforced in the programming of all broadcasting organisations.
- Independent producers should be encouraged to be more creative and promote Nigeria's cultural values in content development.
- Stakeholders (e.g. regulator, broadcasters, educational institutions) should strengthen the collaboration between newsroom and classroom for content enrichment, skills development and feedback.
- Management and infrastructure of the training arm of the broadcast industry should be updated and maintained.

Broadcasting reform efforts

Civil society groups engaged in media issues, broadcasting in particular, should form a working group to assess their reform objectives and strategies with the aim to form a coalition to push effectively for broadcasting reform. Priority should be given to:

- Developing a common policy document which sets out the objectives of reform;
- Initiating public debate on broadcasting issues throughout the country;
- Involving other civil society groups such as faith organisations, trade unions and human rights organisations in their campaigns;
- Lobbying parliament, especially its relevant committees and legislators

who care about human rights and good governance, on the essentials of democratic broadcasting reform;

- continuing dialogue with the executive branch of government (especially the ministry of information and communication) to ensure full adoption of proposed reforms.

www.ingramcontent.com/pod-product-compliance
Lightning Source LLC
Chambersburg PA
CBHW081740270326
41932CB00020B/3352